Meditat

To dearest
TAMIE
in the hope
that one day
you will
return to us,
if not in this
life, in the next

Friedrich Rittelmeyer

Meditation

Guidance of the inner life

Floris Books

Translated by M.L. Mitchell, B.A.

Originally published in German under the title
Meditation. Zwölf Briefe über Selbsterziehung
by Verlag Urachhaus in 1929.
First published in English
by the Christian Community Press, London in 1932
This edition published in 1987 by Floris Books

British Library CIP data available

ISBN 0-86315-065-9

Printed in Great Britain
by Billing & Sons Ltd, Worcester

CONTENTS

INTRODUCTION

HUMANITY is overwhelmed to-day by all kinds of advice regarding meditation. In this is expressed the elementary feeling that the inward powers of man must be strengthened, if he is not to succumb to the force of the outward world.

But what is offered is either outward practical advice about living, with no real feeling for the deep realities of the world, or it springs from a spirituality indeed, but from a spirituality which does not bear within it a strong will directed towards the earth. That which comes from the West, and especially the American West, is mostly of the first kind, but Coué also belongs to it. That which comes from the East, especially from the Indian East, reveals the other kind, but the sentimentalism of Mt. Athos lies also in this direction. Between these, there is offered from the South a training for humanity, which indeed combines spiritual knowledge and practical exercises for daily life, but has not shared the new age's evolution towards perception and freedom, and has caused men to be permeated by the forces of the past: I mean the exercises of the Roman Catholic Church. The intensity of the desire for these exercises, whether in the Jesuitical or other similar forms, again reveals the need of present day humanity.

A way is attempted in these letters which is different from all of these. It is one that would find, in a way suitable to the present time, the Spirit of Christ, which has heaven within it but seeks—the earth. And so it would avoid the dangers of the West and of the East, and also the danger of the past. For the source we shall turn always to the Gospel of St. John. At first this may estrange many who do not yet know what a possession they have in St. John's Gospel. But as we believe this source to offer the best help this cannot be avoided. Everywhere thought has been given to those who approach out of the heathendom of the present day. For complete sincerity and freedom are the first requisites in a spiritual training suitable to this age. This was the expressed conviction of Rudolf Steiner, to whom the author owes all that is best in regard to these things, who had the greatest experience of spiritual development, and who was especially concerned that middle Europe should recognise and fulfil her duty at the right time.

I

THE first of these letters will explain the author's intention. He was led to publish them by the conviction that humanity at the present day is in very great danger. We do not refer to a poison-gas war or a universal catastrophe. These may threaten. But present day Life itself has assumed such forms that humanity is on the way to lose *mankind*.

The disturbing thought is the way in which, day by day, we are claimed and absorbed by our work. This applies especially to those whose work is technical, but in some measure it applies to all. Our work threatens to destroy the human being in us, to make real humanity impossible, to destroy the true future of humanity, yes, even to kill human life itself. Few men see clearly how they are living. They are not really living, they are dwelt in all day long by some unknown power which swings a whip over them. At some early hour of the morning, duty inexorably awakens them. And one duty follows on the heels of another, and all of them hound man on. What kind of a force is it that has become lord over us ?

In those years when my own life resembled this modern life, I was a Protestant vicar in Würzburg, and, besides other duties of preaching and congregational life, I had to give twenty-two lessons a week for seven long years. They were lessons in religion, and of my own free will I had become an enthusiastic servant of religion. But as morning by morning the four hours of religious instruction came round and had to be given, it was as if every joy a human being had in an ideal vocation was being eradicated. If, as a man, one tried to put one's soul into it, one became ill. At that time there hovered over me a picture which may appeal to many men of the present day. I saw that I must every day put on a coat of mail and go about in it. To some extent it bore me up and protected me, but it oppressed the hidden growing *human being* who called for life.

When one frequently says to-day that man is in danger of becoming a machine, one does not take this danger nearly seriously enough. The machine eats its way into our lives from without, and finally devours us and puts itself in our place. This is true not only for ordinary vocations but also for higher, and even for the very highest. For example, there are certain very fine human instruments of precision ; we call them scholars. One of these has admitted that the hours when work gives real joy and life are rare for them also. Research work, when carried on according to the strictest methods, can become mechanical and can make one mechanical, and leave small scope for the free play of the spirit. And how is it with others ? One can already clearly recognise the machine in the faces of many working men and women. There are faces stamped and set in a mould in which the spirit runs, as it were, on rails. One seeks in vain for the glowing life of inexhaustible humanity, for creative fire. The tragedy of man in the machine age is written upon these features.

If one advises such people to cultivate at least some personal interest outside their profession, one receives the answer once given to me by a highly gifted civil engineer : " Yes, I have sometimes tried to do so, but then, when I read a book in the evening after supper, I suddenly remember that I have not read through the latest technical magazines, and that my competitors get ahead of me if I do not devote *all* my time and strength to my profession—and I then lay the book down again." In this way men grow up who no longer know how to use their leisure rightly. Besides sleep and quite stupid rest, sensation is the only recreation. Excitement is sought either in sport or in news of sport; men give themselves up to the nerve-stimulating sensations of the cinema, wireless or revue, or read detective novels, or begin to gamble. One often gets the impression that such men are merely corpses, animated by skilful arts into an appearance of life. The saying in the Act of Consecration of Man concerning the "dying earth-existence," expresses the dreadful background of reality behind the superhuman strain of the present day.

Now and again one experiences how the repressed life of the soul bursts out somewhere forcibly, as if it were making a vent for itself. Then such men suddenly fall into an oppressive mysticism, or into childish sentimentality. They attend spiritualistic seances, and enjoy the thrill of them. They fly into the incense-laden unfathomableness of a Catholic Church, and give themselves up to the emotions they find there. They read foolish poems and learn them by heart. They revel in feelings about nature, without having anything natural about them.

All this may seem to be exaggerated, and so it is if one looks at life in its whole breadth. But it is not exaggerated, no word of it is exaggerated, if one looks at the inner tendency of this life. For what reason has a man been permitted to have intimate dealings for thirty years with all kinds of human fates, if he cannot use his experience to help other men? And so let it be said boldly that behind all this one can often see spiritual sickness coming; not only the death of the soul which Nietzsche describes in his Zarathustra as coming to the "last human being," but demoniac madness.

3

Of all this we shall give but bare indications here. But only when we see clearly the dangers of present day life for ourselves and others, will the effort to build into this life quiet hours for inward strengthening become, not merely an egotistic endeavour or personal dilettantism, but an act of responsibility towards life, a help for threatened humanity, a work of redemption for ourselves and our fellow-men. The readers we would wish to have for these letters are those who are permeated by the thought that man is lost if new strength cannot be brought to him from within, so that he may not be overthrown by the violence from without.

To-day many men feel that a new spirituality must arise if man is to obtain from present conditions an understanding of the world, and press on to solve the riddles of existence. They seek this new spirituality now here, now there, but seldom where it is really to be found.

But a new inner training is also necessary if humanity is to be saved and led on towards a strong future. In earlier centuries men found much comfort and support in the religious conception of the world, in regular cult, in the old spiritualities which still held sway in men's callings and in the sheltered life of the family. All this to-day has fallen, or is falling, to pieces. In those times also the mechanical nature of daily work was not so tyrannical and deadening, except in the case of the lower labouring classes, which vegetated dully. Only when the men of to-day take the training and strengthening of their own selves in hand consciously and energetically throughout their whole lives, will they outgrow this danger which threatens the world.

What is here offered as a help is drawn from the heart of religion, which is the strongest source of power. But let no one be kept away if the truths which will be discussed

4

and from which help will be drawn are for the moment not yet inwardly accessible to him, and therefore, not yet immediately applicable. Let him make his own that which is suited to him.

Everything which is here offered as *content*, may be regarded as merely example, and one may find the *content* which expresses one's own inward spirit in the poets or where one will. Yet everything which is presented here can be serviceable as regards its *form*. Once for all let it be said that there are two essentials if this advice is to bring blessing; they are sincerity and freedom. Only that in respect of which a man can be answerable to his own sincerity, ought he to allow to act upon him. That does not exclude his inward experimental approach to a thought or a truth, if all due precautions are taken; but we must never allow the consciousness to leave us, that we are making an experiment. Anything which we allow to enter us in the nature of a suggestion, even of self-suggestion, would have a destructive effect. It is fundamentally a theft on which punishment follows. The other essential is that one should personally in full freedom work out for oneself what is here offered.

True, they are counsels which come from experience. But the experience of others can illuminate indeed, but not replace, our own experience. He who has gone before us, can tell us that there is a path in this direction and whither that path leads, but that does not release us from the duty of giving heed to the path ourselves and, in certain circumstances, changing our path. The more freely that which is offered here is worked out, the more gain will result, and even when one is able to follow the content verbally, one must at every moment preserve the most perfect freedom within oneself.

I owe most in the sphere which we are about to enter to my teacher, Rudolf Steiner. But I did not first learn the value of inward work on one's own self, the meaning of meditation, from him. I shall thoroughly explain here, how first I came to meditation, because much may be learned from that. When I was an undergraduate, often during the night I had violent attacks of heart beating. I was at my wits' end. Although I knew quite clearly that there was no danger to life, I was in as great a state of anxiety for my life as if I must succumb. I did not consult a doctor, but myself set about finding a means of getting rid of this state. I found help in the resolve to go over in my mind at such times, some pleasant and harmless day of my life.

Only when I succeeded in doing this consecutively without digression and always with my eye on the happy fundamental mood of the day, did it succeed fully. "Now you are getting up; now you are going to the washstand, now you are taking the sponge into your hand. . . . now you are going into another room, now you take a chair from the corner and put it at the table, now you sit down on it, etc. . . ." After a good half-hour I had regained the mastery over my body and could go to sleep. Later when I was in conditions of soul which may be described as attacks of despondency, I helped myself similarly. I thought or lived again through some experience in all its details consecutively, until the ground of my soul-life became firm again and no longer rocked. These examples may serve to show that in cases when many doctors would prescribe sedatives or sick-leave, one can, by one's own will, help oneself by purely spiritual possibilities. In how many illnesses can one bring about a cure, if one understands how to call up in oneself a peaceful, happy, even frame of mind !

This example also shows that it need not always be a weighty cosmic maxim, which is made the soul's content. In many cases one is not in a position to do this. A harm-

6

lessly interesting, perhaps even a quite commonplace succession of pictures, is often a much better help. One feels one's way from picture to picture as from one bar of a railing to the next. One gives attention to each step, as if one were going along a narrow path, and had time to look around one. If this does not succeed, and if we catch our thoughts wandering, we recall ourselves, as soon as we notice this, to the path, without becoming unduly agitated about ourselves and our weaknesses. We learn gradually.

From Rudolf Steiner I later learned the value of succeeding in seeing oneself from without, if one daily devotes at least a few moments to looking at one's life throughout the past day from without and from above ; how one thereby prepares oneself for the backward look at life from beyond death. According to Rudolf Steiner, this is best done if one tries to go backwards over the course of the day either in whole or in part, not in order to become a spiritual acrobat, as captious critics say, but because one thereby sees much more clearly the inward course of one's life, just as, also, after death, one looks backwards and reviews the course of one's life. I knew nothing of all that at the time. I only found that such a method of meditation was beneficial to my life, and to the training of the spirit. One learned to lay hold of one's spirit, and knew that it was well for one so to cultivate inner control.

Then, as a young theologian, I found the value of religious meditation and the quiet hour. My experiences at that time, and the advice I gave to many are spoken of in the sermon, " On Being Alone," in the book " God and Soul," which appeared in the year 1906, long before my first contact with Anthroposophy.

Yet my first clear insight into this whole sphere, and my first consciously directed effort towards a definite goal,

7

came through Rudolf Steiner. Simple truth and gratitude demand that I should acknowledge it. And, as I think back, I regard it as remarkable that in my very first talk with Rudolf Steiner, without my having said the least thing about it either to himself or to others from whom he might have heard it, he began to talk about meditation and gave me advice about it.

So that no misunderstandings or uncertainties may arise, I must now clearly distinguish between what Dr. Steiner could do in this sphere, and the advice he could give, and what it is possible to do in these letters. There are many misconceptions prevalent about Rudolf Steiner and his spiritual exercises; therefore a word about them will be welcome to many. As far as I could observe, Dr. Steiner gave meditations of about seven different kinds :—

1. He recommended people who came to him to meditate upon some saying or sequence of sayings taken from the Bible. In this way he directed many people to the beginning of the Gospel of John. In lectures which he gave soon after the beginning of his active work, he declared that if anyone would take the first five verses of the Gospel of John earnestly into his soul regularly every morning for even five minutes, in the course of a year his whole inward life would be changed. As far as I know such meditations were given to people who were inclined to religion. Dr. Steiner pointed to Russians especially in this direction. The first mighty sentences of John's Gospel can above all serve to give a man a cosmic depth, dignity and rhythm in life which are a great benefit amid its manifold distracting details.

2. Rudolf Steiner gave general meditations, such as are published in his " Wahrspruchworte " (verses or 'true sayings') or are found in his Mystery Plays. They are directed more to men who come from the life

8

of the present day, and do not, like the meditations on John's Gospel, pre-suppose an inward attraction towards the Bible, but they always lead into the central depths.

In all the meditations given by him, Rudolf Steiner laid especial stress upon vowel sound and rhythm and upon the sequences of the thoughts and words, and he said emphatically that nothing in the actual form of such sentences was unimportant.

Many of these meditations, which were given more to members of the Anthroposophical Society, pre-suppose an acquaintance with the truths of Spiritual Science. Other sayings are related to individual circumstances or relationships, such as those on relationship to the dead, or to children, or to the sick, or to soldiers at the front, or for meal times, etc. Others were given for meditation to people of special rank in life.

3. Rudolf Steiner gave to individual people numerous meditations which were specially composed for them. These sayings will probably, for the most part, never be known. For those who received them treasure them as life-long possessions intended for and entrusted to them personally. If one happens to get a look into the world of this advice, one is astonished at its fullness and many-sidedness, at its suitability to individual cases, and at the loving care shown here to men.

4. If it were a question of training for development, Rudolf Steiner gave hints how man could work at his own spiritual development for the sake of the future of humanity. Such advice has been made public in his books, " Knowledge of the Higher Worlds and its Attainment " and " An Outline of Occult Science." Exercises for the control of the thoughts and feelings and for the education of the will, and also the Rosicrucian Meditation, are given in the " Outline of Occult Science" (1939 Edn., pp. 230-232).

5. During the last year of his activity, Rudolf Steiner was much engaged in special work for a selected circle of Anthroposophists at the " High School for Spiritual Science," at Dornach. The aim of this activity was to further the birth of spirit man in the sense of the age of Michael.

6. If Rudolf Steiner considered that individual people, by reason of their gifts and their fate, were fitted to be brought into closer connection with the revelations of the Spiritual World, he gave them spiritual exercises which formed a complete system suited to these individual people. If this is mentioned here, it is only in order to establish two facts in the face of all perversions and slanders. (1) These exercises contain no other secrets than those publicly answered for in Rudolf Steiner's lectures and writings. (2) They preserve most carefully the inner freedom, and, by Rudolf Steiner's express will, are to be adapted and worked out quite freely by each individual according to his needs.

7. For the direct development of the spiritual organs of perception described in his book " Knowledge of the Higher Worlds and its Attainment," Rudolf Steiner very seldom gave advice, and then only to very few people, under strict preliminary moral conditions. To this advice also, all that was said in the previous paragraph is applicable. These people have certainly not progressed so far that they can confirm by their own experience all the researches of Rudolf Steiner. They have all, without exception, found that the way is longer and harder than they thought at the beginning. But among them and with them there are not a few Anthroposophists who have made the beginnings of discoveries in the most different spheres, and can rightly say, " The world of which Rudolf Steiner tells does exist ; we know from our own impressions to what a large extent what he said has

been proved true. A proof that here there can be no talk of suggestion or of auto-suggestion is just this—that, in spite of all our efforts, there is much that we have *not* attained, and that what we did attain was always different from what we had expected, and yet has confirmed what Rudolf Steiner told us."

Of the above mentioned seven possibilities for meditation, only the first can be considered here. Those who are interested in the rest must apply to the Anthroposophical Society or to individual Anthroposophists. Exercises like those named under 3, 6, and 7, can be given scientifically only when a person's whole manner of being can be looked at with the eyes of a true seer.

And since Rudolf Steiner's death, there is no one who, to my knowledge, can possibly do this, certainly not the writer of these letters. But we may say that the Biblical meditations of which we shall here speak, can not only train a man morally but bring him much further upon the way towards the spiritual future than one thinks when entering upon them at first. Even he who cannot look at himself and at men with the eyes of a seer will soon become certain that he is upon the right spiritual path when he follows the hints given in this, the highest of human records.

The Bible was given to humanity by the divine guiding powers, not for hurried reading, but to be worked at inwardly. It contains, in fact, the path to all spiritual heights of humanity. It ought to be made part of humanity's own life—in a much more thorough, and also a freer, way than ever in the past. We shall attempt to do this here, when, in the formation of the separate meditations, we apply the inspiration and experience which have been won through Anthroposophy.

Now that we have thus drawn a distinction between our work and the Anthroposophical activity of

Dr. Steiner, we must place it in the right relationship to the activity of the Christian Community. The great undertaking of the Christian Community unites men by a cult celebrated in common. Anyone who lets the Christian cult serve in any way as a help in his life is a member with full rights. He may shape his inner life in quite a different way from that here explained. In the working out of the Act of Consecration of Man, in personal prayer, especially in the Lord's Prayer, he can find all that he needs. Each man is left completely free, even in the way in which he inwardly makes his own the cult in the celebration of which he shares.

What is done here is not done officially from the Christian Community. It is, therefore, possible that those who find difficulties in regard to the cult, or who for other reasons do not wish to be more closely connected with the organisation of the Christian Community, may find that they can share in this. These letters are written for every man who wishes for help in the cultivation of his inner life and is willing to hear what is offered to him in this way in the world of Christianity.

It will help perception and understanding if we point out here the inward connection between meditation and cult. One may say frankly that a meditation is rightly constructed when its inward course is like the course of the Act of Consecration of Man. Besides all else which the Act of Consecration of Man is, it may also be regarded as a great meditation in common, carried out not by the purely personal human being, but by the earthly human being ; not by the isolated individual man, but by the man typical of humanity ; not by the subjective egotistical man, but by the Christ-man.

Conversely, right meditation may be understood as an act of consecration performed not in the outer world, but in the world within ; not in the community, but in solitude; not in the world of the priest, but in one's own thoughts. Each must decide for himself what helps him most or whether perhaps the one helps the other. It is certain that to look at the Act of Consecration of Man, even at its details, but still more at its inward course and attitude, gives most valuable indications of the right construction of meditation.

Let the first attempt to recommend a meditation, or, let us say, to indicate an effective content for the work of our quiet hours, be undertaken in connection with the four parts of the Act of Consecration of Man.

We choose the saying from the Epistles of John, in which Johannine Christianity is summed up : *God is love, and he that dwelleth in love, dwelleth in God, and God in him.*

In order to shape the meditation as a unity and comprehensively, let us direct our attention to the first sentence : God is love. He for whom this saying has not yet the full weight of a truth may choose some other thought, such as the sentence : Love is the meaning of this earthly world ; or, still more reticently : Pure Love is one of the aims of human life. On the other hand, he who finds the truths of Christianity to be the ultimate realities may strengthen the saying by thinking it to be spoken by Christ Himself : I am Love. If these words were not actually spoken by Christ, yet they are the content of His life and radiate from it.

Our aim is *to attain the spiritual content of such a saying as strongly as possible within us for some time.* We must first get beyond mere thinking round such a saying. The man of to-day usually finds this very difficult; he begins to reflect when he ought to meditate. For very thinking he cannot reach the spirit. Or if he succeeds in dismissing those will-o-the-wisps, his thoughts, he sinks into the world of pure feeling, luxuriates in it and calls it mysticism. Both errors must be overcome. One can do this if one develops a certain inner activity beyond pure thought. Only through such activity is it possible for one to make such a thought one's own for a quarter-of-an-hour, without becoming dulled and falling into a helpless brooding upon it.

One man may find it good, perhaps, in order to make the word " love " become living within him in the right way, to seek in his memories for the time when love met him in its purest and highest form. Let him look at such an experience, seeing only the nature of the love, the spirit of the love, which revealed itself to him. One does not need consciously to hold fast the feeling which is thus awakened in one, but one can always make the word " love " live again, by thinking back for a moment ; such a being, only much purer, more spiritual, more perfect—is God, is Christ.

In order to become inwardly sufficiently active, and yet not to lose one's way in pure thinking, one may represent to oneself, and try to repeat in one's feelings, how this word shines out in the soul of the disciple John as a great revelation ; how it is made living for him by the remembrance of that which he has experienced in Christ, how it is felt by him, in contrast to the whole ancient world which surrounds him. Such efforts will become very dear to a man. They will raise him above the egotism of ordinary Christianity. One shares, as well as one can, in the great revelation of God, which then dawned in the soul of man. Naturally, if we then suddenly catch ourselves allowing all sorts of recollections of our reading about the exuberant life of the Roman Empire to ebb and flow in our soul, we have gone astray. We must look only at the central truth, and make it alive in every way we can.

Another very effective way of making the word strong within us, may be to imagine the word being spoken to us from all the breadths of the world, from all the heights of heaven. It resounds in higher and higher choirs of angels ; it is like the hidden music of the world, which, in spite of all evil and need, sounds forth out of divine kingdoms. We listen to this music until it becomes our own soul.

Again, another way to make the saying our own, may be to imagine to oneself the end of the earth's development. Here is a multitude of men to whom this secret has been revealed, in whom this word lives as their own soul. In them, redeemed humanity looks up to the Divine Father of the world, and brings to Him its confession of Christ. Men much better and greater than we, are there, but we also are among them. As in the mirror of these human souls, the Godhead sees itself and rejoices. Men who doubt the fact of a divine love which bears the world, can yet,without sentimentality, call to life within them such an end as being the goal of humanity.

One can choose for oneself one of these three ways of making the word great and powerful, as suits one best, or one can let all three pass one after the other through one's soul, the past, the present, the future—and can remain at each picture as long as is possible without much deviation from it.

All that has been said up till now corresponds to the first part of the Act of Consecration of Man : the proclamation of the Gospel. The helps which we have suggested, and which can also be obtained in other ways, are intended to keep us from a full surrender to our feelings, and lead us to a spiritual feeling. Divine love, the great truth which is the background of the world, must be brought to a clarity and a power which correspond to its place in the kingdom of truth.

One might stop at this point, and strive only for the attainment of this first thing. Then everything else would also take place along with it, unconsciously. But, if the meditations are to become more actively living, the following must now take place :—

Let us now hold fast in our souls, as long and as strongly as possible, not an individual detail of the pictures, but only their great chief impression. Now, however, we turn our attention more inwardly upon ourselves. Here, again, the contemplation of pictures will help to keep the inward activity awake and living. For without inward activity, nothing can be done. Let us, therefore, represent this saying of John, as a clear altar flame, burning inwardly in our souls. Our whole being comes to the altar from all sides, and offers itself to this divine fire. We give to this fire our thinking, our feeling, our willing successively. We seek so fully to pass away in this divine fire as if we ourselves were no longer there, and the whole space in which we had lived, were filled by this divine fire. Then we seek to come to life again in this divine fire with our conscious, pure ego. We strive that our ego should glow and shine in this fire alone.

So we sacrifice our ego to the fire of Christ, and we try to listen to Christ's saying in us : " I am love," and we seek to gain a new ego from Him. We try to leave behind us our whole life up to the present, to hear the voice of Christ in a divine world above the earth, as He speaks out of the purest spirit of love : " No one taketh My life, I give it. This new commandment have I from My Father, that I lay down My life for the brethren." And we seek in this spirit to return into life. We seek to make this ego, illuminated by Christ, become so strong that it glows through three circles, first through ourselves, completely through our being and life, then through the whole circle of men among whom we live, and lastly, as far as possible, through the whole world.

All these efforts are not attempts at "self-redemption,"

as is again and again mistakenly asserted, but only endeavours to fit oneself for that which is ready for us, and to fit oneself for it with the earnestness which befits the loftiness and greatness of this gift of revelation.   Or they are not even attempts to fit oneself, but attempts to be ready for it and to give oneself to it in return.   Man will soon find that one thing he cannot do—sacrifice himself.   He will grasp ever more clearly the reason why a real religious service contains within itself sacrifice as a special part of it, because man requires a special training in sacrifice

Even in the smallest details, man can here also draw enabling power, help and advice for meditation, from that which happens in the second part of the Act of Consecration of Man, from the offering.   He will understand more and more clearly how Rudolf Steiner could say that man, if he wishes to reach true revelation out of the Divine World, must learn to develop powers of devotion far surpassing any he requires in ordinary life.

One may apply as one will the hints given here, the goal is ever the same, that our ego may be filled with the fire of the spirit, which is no feeble flickering, but purest, warmest light of man's being, which streams and glows in us out of the depths of the world.

If he succeeds in doing this ever more strongly, man will make all kinds of discoveries.   He will for the first time really discover what he could be and ought to be, and what he is not.   He will find how far removed his whole being is from the Divine Being.   He will now really see, for the first time, and will feel in a more living way the distance between God and Man.   For he knows, not from history, nor from dogma, but from his own experience what the fall of man is.   He learns by experience that not only is his spirit unable to live steadily in this world, but that his body and his whole life struggle

17

against the constant indwelling of such truth. He feels very strongly in every limb of his body that he is corrupt. And yet a man could not have such an experience, nor could he bear it, if he did not feel within himself a power of another kind, which seeks to transform him, and which can transform him.

Out of the word of truth streams into us the force, the divine creative power, which makes another man of us. It is an incredibly slow process to change not only the consciousness, but the whole being as well. One has the impression that one is working upon a stone, not with a chisel but with water. But a man looks not at what he is, but at what he shall be, and feels that he is changing.

Then also, moments come when he really becomes one with such a word of revelation. For one holy moment the divine word itself becomes his life. He receives the communion, and, strengthened through it as through miraculous food, he returns into his earthly existence. We have experienced within us transubstantiation and communion as it is accomplished at the altar for the celebrating community.

If we now look at the saying of John as it is delivered to us, look at its own inward course, we can say—in the sentence—" *God* is love," we are more in the first part of the Act of Consecration of Man, and of meditation. The more we lay emphasis upon the second part of the sentence, " God is *love*," the more we are drawn into the second part, into the offering. With the sentence, " And he who dwells in love, dwells in God," we can feel ourselves in the third part, in the transubstantiation ; " And God in him," that is the communion. No outward thoughts of the Apostle arranged it so. But such Bible sayings are often built up according to an inner law, such as lies at the root of a right cult, and such as, in meditation, is felt to be right and beneficial and necessary.

18

With this meditation, or let us say again, with this spiritual content of quiet hours, which may well also become a prayer in the soul, we have laid the foundation for a whole organism of inner exercises, by which we may call the Johannine Christianity to life within us. The author has now only this to say, that these letters must infallibly become wearisome if the reader does not from the beginning take an inwardly active share in what is here attempted. On no account let him be held off or perplexed by difficulties or lack of success. Nothing is so certain of reward as that which is done rightly for the inner life. A circle of people may be formed who are working earnestly at themselves in a religious sense, who will form the nucleus of renewal, and who are working from their inmost beings against humanity's great present dangers.

II

WHEN Francis took leave of Mount Alverno, upon which he had received the stigmata, he cast a last glance back towards the sacred heights. He kneeled down and said, " Farewell, thou mountain of God, thou Holy Mountain ; *mons coagulatus, mons pinguis, mons in quo bene placitum est Deo habitare ;* farewell, Mount Alverno, may God the Father, God the Son and God the Holy Ghost bless thee ; peace be with thee for we shall see one another no more."

He who is alive to the soul of words like these can feel what the still places of prayer meant in the soul of Francis and what the man of to-day lacks. Where now has man his mount of worship ? An impression from nature, upon a lonely mountain height at sunrise, is the last dying whisper of the memory of that which the men of past ages felt upon their mountain tops. We must regain that which echoes in such sayings of Francis, if the very best is not to be lost from humanity.

Solovieff speaks in one place of the " inner Athos " which every man must have. The spirit of Russia in him looks back to the sacred mountain in Greece, from which so much blessing has streamed out over Russia. But Solovieff knows also that the past does not return. The man of to-day must found his own cloister within himself. This is true in a very much wider sense than one imagines. This longing for the cloister in many men comes from deep reasons. But were we to flee to the Roman Catholic cloisters, we should find a world other than that which we expected, a world in which we could no longer feel at home. Even at the best we should admit to ourselves that our longing had been for something different from what we found there. But in the Protestant church this call for the foundation of evangelical cloisters has largely died away. It was really a misunderstanding. The call for the cloister is born out of inner need. But it means something other than men themselves think. It really calls for that which we are trying to do here. What is here taking place is the founding of an order. But each must build his cloister within himself; out of freedom in solitude. Those who belong to such an order may indeed sometimes meet or talk with one another. But what is most important comes in being alone. All the cloisters of the past are prophecies of that which must happen within the soul.

But let us return from the Catholic to the Biblical picture. When, in John's Gospel, the Samaritan woman points Christ to Mount Gerazim and its sanctuary, Christ speaks words full of meaning for the future : " God is Spirit, and they that worship Him must worship Him in spirit and in truth, for the Father seeketh such to worship Him." The mountain of which Christ speaks is within, and He calls it " the spirit." The temple of which He speaks is invisible ; it stands upon no spot of earth, and He calls it " the truth." The mountain of the spirit, upon which stands the temple of truth, is what we seek. We want to build it within us as an " inner Athos," as " the sacred Mount Alverno." And when we go to men and to our daily work, then shall we " come down from the mountain." Once when Christ came down from the mountain, with the glory in which He dwelt there shining around Him, His disciples entreated Him : " Lord, teach us to pray ; to pray as thou canst pray." When we are able to rouse in men longings for the mountain of the temple from which we draw our strength, then shall we be the healers of our age.

Rudolf Steiner once said that if this hurried, external

life of ours continues for a few more decades, the children will be born already trembling. Such words can most forcibly impress upon our souls the seriousness of the mission which we have to ourselves and to our times.

The " truth " of which Christ speaks, is a great kingdom which we must first discover for ourselves. One can find it only when one has the quality which corresponds to it, that is : sincerity. If one suggests to oneself a thought to which one has no inward right, one takes a destructive element into one's soul. That is why it is so misleading when Coué can recommend to mankind as a meditation, " Every day, in every way, I get better and better." One may, of course, attain something by such meditation, as one may often cure a disease by simply ignoring it, or as in Christian Science circles by simply treating illness in humanity as if it did not exist. Yet the tendency of this is false and dangerous and its failure to preserve entire truthfulness to the facts must somewhere and somehow lead to a relapse. It would be better to meditate thus : " I wish that it should go better with me," or " I wish that the illness may be overcome." Then we need only ask further if such a representation to oneself of one's bodily condition and health does not overlook still deeper associations with reality, and invite into one's inner life spirits of egoism and materialism, which may indeed help against the evil of the moment, but later demand a worse penalty. We have the right to defend ourselves against every illness. But true insight knows also that every illness is meant to bring its own blessing into the house, for the soul and, as Anthroposophical Science conclusively shows, for the body also. We ought to let no illness depart from us without our having wrung from it its blessing. One can apply to it exactly the old saying : " I will not let thee go except thou bless me."

That for which we are here striving bears within itself bodily health also. But this is spread through the body through the soul's becoming healthy. This feeling of becoming healthy ought to occur after every right meditation. "Through Thy word my soul becomes whole," says the Act of Consecration of Man. For my part I must admit that I never rightly knew what health meant until I experienced it through meditation. A real feeling of health permeates soul and body. Some may think they know this feeling after a strenuous mountain climb or vigorous exercise in a game. The feeling described here is similar, only very much more spiritual. And in this way one feels oneself safe, and in the long run gets further than by curing oneself of some particular illness by auto-suggestion.

From such false advice men have come to think that every meditation is self-suggestion. It is no more and no less so than if a man should undertake to master his temper, or to bear a pain, or to behave decently to someone else. By accusing it of being auto-suggestion, one can throw suspicion on every effort of the will. One can even forbid any kind of influence exercised by teachers upon children, because it may be suggestion. In reality the question is whether that to which one wishes to give the mastery in one's soul is a truth or an ideal which one has understood, and which one may safely make a lasting possession. In the very nature of suggestion and auto-suggestion is implicit an unreality which one would like to press upon oneself and others, or at least the unlawful interference with another's freedom. Through such confused conceptions it comes about that men do not trust themselves to exert their wills against their natural instincts at that moment in their history when it is all-important that they should learn to do so, in order to remain human, and even to become human. Concerning the exercises of the soul which are here recommended, one can only repeat that they should be practised only in the land of truth and freedom. In it even the strongest will can bring no harm, but will be a real help and benefit.

So that we may first learn the value of inward occupation with oneself from exercises which everyone who comes to them from without can share, let us here discuss fully such a preliminary exercise. But first it is well to reply to a question often asked by beginners : " What bodily attitude is best for meditation ? "

Certainly the bodily attitude is not unimportant. And from the body difficulties arise, which we shall discuss more fully later. The Eastern man brought his body to rest by sitting down upon his crossed legs. But, apart from the fact that we are unaccustomed to such a position and assume it only with difficulty, it cuts men off from certain currents which pass from the earth into the body. By such a bodily position the Oriental man assists his striving away from the earth, which striving is the content of his meditation and the spirit of his view of the world. We see almost exactly the opposite of this in Western man, who for centuries has prayed upon his knees. In such a bodily position man is outwardly nearer to the earth, but he receives the earth influences, though naturally quite gently and unconsciously, yet more strongly into himself. This occurs the more readily, as we indeed can feel, because the feet have much more spirituality of their own than the knees have. We feel them in a much more living way. Therefore, when we kneel, we unite ourselves still more closely with that which streams forth from the earth, and also by kneeling to pray, the mission of the West to the earth is prepared and furthered.

And now what is our position ? For us, it is not right to allow ourselves to be supported by any natural spiritual force whatsoever, which we do not understand, but we must seek the higher world out of a clear consciousness and out of a free will. Therefore, there is only one rule for us : our natural bodily existence must disturb us as little as possible. The position in which our spirit feels itself as little disturbed as possible, is best for us. One can find this out only by experiment. One man requires greater comfort, which makes another man go to sleep. The other requires a more rigid posture, which would distract the first. One can only say : " As much comfort as is possible without laziness."

The meditation of which we are now about to speak is an aid to acquiring calmness of spirit. It is so arranged that it is of especial benefit to the man of the present day in his hurried life, and at the same time shows how one can rise to the very highest from what is quite simple.

Let us simply turn our attention to the word " Rest." At a time when the quiet life of the hermit is common, it would not be good to choose it, but, in the age of incessant haste, it may be to innumerable people a rare benefit to body and soul to come to be at home with this word " Rest."

Here again the treasures of remembrance must come to our aid. Where, in my past life, did I most strongly experience what rest is ? We think of a quiet evening in a wood. We sat upon a seat by a lake. The waves rippled gently at our feet. The trees rustled almost imperceptibly in the evening wind. Twilight spread itself like a sheltering garment over the land. That day we had done our full measure of work. Now we had rest at evening.

The more living and concrete the picture is, the better. When we have called the picture strongly to life, then we dismiss it and retain only the feeling ; the feeling of a great refreshing peace filling all around.

What an evening in a wood is to one man, the

impression made by high mountains with eternal snows may be to another, as he saw them quite suddenly, far before him in the distance, as he went on an expedition, like an unfathomable premonition of a higher world. And still another may recall the starry heavens, as they made their strong impression upon him when he came out from some stormy public meeting or lively private assembly. Some may also have had a like experience from Goethe's *Abendlied* : " *Ueber allen Gipfeln ist Ruh*," or from some other poem of the evening. It is always important that all the details of one's recollection should serve only as a help to reaching a feeling of great rest.

This rest must be felt as strongly as possible. We may say to ourselves in such a case : " You have now a strong feeling of rest, but there are certainly people who feel it ten times as strongly as you do." It is not only necessary in this meditation, which may last from five to fifteen minutes, to continue to hold fast to this rest as consciously as possible, and at the same time to assent to it inwardly, but it is also necessary to let it become ever stronger, as far as this is possible, and to fill the whole body with it and to pour forth the body with it. We may also, in order to remain inwardly active, bring our limbs to rest one by one. Then we will notice how much tension there is in our limbs, in our hands, our feet, our brain and in the neck muscles which carry our head. We look upon rest as a drink which flows throughout all the kingdom of the body.

Certainly some will say " That would send me to sleep," and is it such a bad thing if one has a means of going to sleep ? This meditation may help him to sleep, who finds it hard to do so. He relaxes himself in it. He goes around his body like a watchman round a house and sees what is unwilling to sleep and brings it to rest. Especially there, where the head joins the body, it is well to see that everything is right, so that the head may be quite relaxed. One lets " rest " really rest within one. If a man really wishes it, he may even in apparently difficult cases, go to sleep by means of the exercise ; but he will often notice that he is not really willing to do so, rather that he is in love with his disturbed thoughts and feelings, and will on no account give them up for such a rest. But if he really cannot get to sleep by these means, yet the rest which fills him when he really ceases to think of particular things and rests only in this rest, may be also as beneficial as a real sleep. If anyone is trying to find rest at night in sleep, I would advise him as far as possible to make himself a part of the following picture : Here I rest upon my bed, around me are the walls of the house, but outside is the procession of the stars ; stars are above me, stars are around me, stars are under me ; I should see them through the earth, had I the eyes. The walls of the house, the whole house around me is passing away, even the earth itself is passing away, but that which lives in the stars, remains. I give myself to it, I go out among the stars, I share myself among them until nothing of myself remains here, all is outside with the stars. I move along with them in their courses, slowly, calmly, majestically, eternally. . . .

He who knows Anthroposophical Spiritual Science will know that in this way, with our conscious wills, we go to meet that which sleep requires of us. Such a rest can be of inexpressibly great benefit to us, and when we know it we might almost choose to sleep no more. But if, after this conception of a picture, we can come to the conception of a voice and hear the whole heaven of stars singing this song of praise : " Glory to God in the Highest, and on earth peace to men of good will," and if we can further retain the living feeling which lies at the root of this conception of sound, can keep the sacred

27

spirit of peace, which turns in praise to the heavenly Father, the joyful heavenly rest, the restful joy of heaven, as one keeps a taste upon one's tongue, and can have it throughout our whole being, then we are really with the angels, and can spiritualise and transfigure our sleep in a way of which we have not had hitherto even a distant idea.

But, throughout, we have to do, not with the ability to sleep, but really with the ability to awake. As one can imagine eyes which see by day the starry heaven which is always around us, there can at least be a spirit which dives down so deeply into peace of soul that he feels deep within him that the starry heaven is above him by day also. The spirit of the stars, as we may call it, accompanies him upon his life's way.

As one can take in rest like a medicine, so one can, of course, take into oneself all other possible spiritual contents. An especially health-giving exercise is : Purity. One can build it up and shape it in the same way as we have done with Rest. In this, it may help us to plunge ourselves into the innocent life-stream of the plants, or into the crystal pure glory of a snowy land-scape, or the picture of the Sistine Madonna, or again, the heaven of stars. In the same way a man can learn to draw into himself strength of will, sincerity, kindness. He will find that a great spiritual store of healing, which he can never exhaust, is at his disposal.

If we turn back to the exercise on Rest, it can present itself to him as a sanatorium, which he has built for him-self. He does not require long and costly journeys into the mountains when he wants rest and refreshment. He enters into his own rest. At first, I often imagined to myself that I lived in this rest, as a diver stays under a great glass bell in the sea. Outside the waves pass, the fish go by, the sharks and other sea pirates seek their prey, but he is safely sheltered in his transparent house from which he looks out at what is around him. Thus may a man look out in spirit from his house of rest upon the noise and haste outside. So one can strengthen the feeling of rest by contrast.

Many people will in such ways gradually learn what rest really is. Up till now they have known it only in the form of unconscious sleep. Rest itself passes into us, rests in us, awake and living, feeds us, heals us, makes us divine. When I first experienced that, I had the feeling that now, at last, I saw the possibility of doing something for " nerves." As we can lift a load if we can get a grip beneath it, so now we find a realm which lies below the nerves, and we need only think of the word Rest, and we are already in our house of rest. In the worst of street noises, in the most excited meeting, if we only think of it, Rest rises up like a temple and receives us into its peace.

When we put this into words, we are working at the spiritual life of humanity like a nerve specialist. No drug will help men like these exercises in rest. If humanity would only take seriously what is here written, the danger of neurasthenia and of other worse mental illnesses, which arise from distracting haste, would be overcome in a few decades.

In this study, we have, up to now, spoken in such a way that even the man who is furthest from religion can accompany us. In conclusion, let something more be added out of the world of which religion speaks. Let him who finds grounds for it in his life, change this rest into a great and complete trustfulness. Let him look up to the spirit which rules behind and above all the starry worlds, and permit the peace, which streams to him from afar, to flow back in a great, deep, perfect trustfulness of heart. He will then notice that, in so doing, very much within him will be relaxed which he did not even know was strained. He will be able to " re-act away " much hidden anxiety and fear, without first bringing it by psychoanalytical methods fully into his consciousness. Only it must be a living trust which does not sink down into a fatalistic resignation. For the man of to-day needs the power of active world-conquest. Resignation has been reached by many men of the past. That which is told of Roman Stoics and still more of Buddhist monks, and especially of Buddha himself, arouses reverence before these heights of self-trained humanity, but it is not yet Christian peace.

Therefore it is good here also to look at Christ. Is He not the Word ; the Word for the world ? Does not that which spoke to us out of all the depths of the starry heaven, sound forth also from Him ? Is not the angels' song of praise upon that holy night really His own being echoing forth ? In His farewell discourse Christ said to His disciples, " These words have I spoken unto you that in Me ye might have peace : in the world ye shall have tribulation, but be of good cheer, I have over-come the world." And this other word, " Peace I leave with you, My peace I give unto you, not as the world giveth give I unto you." This word of Christ is found in the Act of Consecration of Man, as it was also in the ancient Mass. In the former it is born again out of His innermost spirit in the words : " I am at peace with the world. This peace with the world can be with you also because I give it to you." And after the resurrection Christ greets His disciples in words full of meaning : " The peace be with you." One may think of this word as spoken once in the past of Christ's history. But one can also think of it as spoken out of the present, as it is every evening in the starry sky, when the revelation of the highest and most divine Spirit is seeking for our souls. If we experience this out of the greatness of the universe, then there is no danger, either that our peace will be merely personal, as so easily happens in a religion of forgiveness of sins, or that we should remain in passive peace, as so easily happens in a religion of trusting in God. But the stern progress of the great world-clock there outside is in sympathy with our inmost feelings. And that is why it is there. Then we are at peace with the world, but we make ourselves one with its progress, as that can come about through Christ. " *My* peace," says Christ with emphasis in John's Gospel. That means, the peace which is I. From that we receive authority to hear Him speaking to us also : " I am the peace. The peace which is I, be with thee ! " If one can so experience the meditation on Rest that one hears the voice of Christ Himself out of all breadths, depths and heights, then one has carried it upward to the greatness and divine power which can be attained by men.

The reader will now wish to ask : Yes, but which meditation ought we then to pursue, that on Love, suggested in the first letter, or this on Peace, which is here suggested ? Such questions will become more urgent for many when we discuss a whole series of other meditations in the following studies, from which it will, we hope, become more and more clear what meditation is and is intended to be. The fact is that one cannot, in advice given in letters, name for everyone the exact meditation which is suited to him. Therefore we can here develop only an organism of inward exercises in which lives the whole Gospel of John. Out of it each must choose that which is right for him. But he may also choose the whole of it, and then his life-work may be to make it inwardly his own. He is upon a good path. For the spirit of John's Gospel, which is so near to the spirit of the coming age, lives in all its fullness in this organism. But we must always keep our eyes fixed upon the central saying which sums up all : "I am Love." We shall unfold the meaning of this saying as we proceed to experience this " I " in the seven "I ams," and then look on " Love" in its divine revelation, in the seven stages of the passion, and lastly see, in the seven miracles of John's Gospel, the " am " in its actual earthly life, and receive it into ourselves.

But the words "I am Peace," which we are considering to-day, are as a background to this. I can imagine a reader finding that he first requires peace more in the sense of John's Gospel ; then he might so meditate that he lets peace sound out until it dies away into love, so that it can be no selfish and passive peace, but the peace "which unites itself with the world's evolving." Another might prefer to remain at the word " love." Then he might first let the word " peace " sound out so that love acquires the greatness, the purity, the rest of the cosmic background, out of which it came with Christ, and so does not lose itself in unhealthy worries or in human pettiness. For the " world's evolving through Christ," of which the Act of Consecration of Man speaks, comes out of " being at peace " with the world.

But we can also think as follows. We take the word "peace " in the evening, so that it passes away into "love," and the word "love " in the morning, so that it proceeds out of " peace." We can let the word " love " arise over us with the sun and the new day; just as we hear the word " peace " resound from the starry heavens and the sheltering night. A great rhythm comes into our life, like the rhythm of day and night, which, indeed, bears within itself the very spirit of this rhythm. This is like a daily divine breathing. A breathing-in when we meditate upon the word " peace," a breathing-out when we meditate upon the word " love." It is like a going out from, and returning into the Father, which corresponds to the hidden rhythm of the life of Christ Himself, as it is shown to us in the Gospel in His day and His night life. Yes, this rhythm lies deep in the background of the proclamation of Christ Himself, as it is given to us in John's Gospel. " I come from the Father," says the first part; " I go to the Father," says the second part. And so we learn in these two meditations to take Christ into our life, as He is described to us by His nearest disciples and friends. Yes, Anthroposophical Spiritual Science tells us that the great divine life bears within itself its mighty and solemn rhythm, since ever, after a world-day of a million years, there comes an evening of rest for the world, when the world returns to God, to come forth from him again newer and greater. With the words " love " and " peace " we come as near as is humanly possible to this rhythm in the life of the Father God.

And let us not keep silence about one secret more, even if to most of our readers it is only like a tale that is told. If our being bathes itself in peace, in harmony with the deepest powers of the cosmos, then gently and inwardly another body builds itself up for us out of the cosmos. If love, the divine spirit of the cosmos, streams through our being, our blood is actually renewed. And therefore in this twin meditation one can experience the highest communion and receive from Christ, to whom we may ever look as far as we may understand Him, His body and His blood.

This is the highest to which we can rise by meditation, that we should simply look into Christ, pass into Him, learn to be in Him and live in Him. To make this possible for men, in all its life and fullness, is the purpose of these studies. Man can feel himself as if enfolded in Christ, breathe in Him as in a higher air, awake as in a higher light, arise as in a higher body.

33

III

MANY people wish for an answer to the question : How is meditation related to prayer ? Not very long ago there appeared an article by the Marburg theologian, Friedrich Heiler, in which we were asked to choose whether we want meditation or prayer. If we were to choose the former we should sink back into Buddhism. Only prayer was really Christian.

In this way of thinking the greatest Christians of the Middle Ages would be expelled from Christianity, for they have really meditated upon the death and resurrection of Christ in a way quite similar to that here recommended. And they owe their wonderful religious strength to the power of their meditation.

Naturally, it is not our opinion that anyone who is accustomed to say his prayers morning and evening should now give up prayer and put meditation in its place. But if an inquiry were held into the subject, one would learn that the number of people who no longer pray is terribly great. They go through life, have now and then by chance childish and usually superstitious thoughts about the higher world, and never notice what they miss. The frightful carelessness and demoralisation which has seized upon the inner lives of men is, as a rule, not realised in religious circles. A course, like this, of instruction in meditation, must include a discussion with those who expect everything from prayer. However, even to look at those who still pray is not encouraging. One can, indeed, never fully know. And occasionally an impression shows us that there is greater reality than one had thought. But how many who pray still do so out of real inward need, and not from custom or superstitious fear ? How many pray from joy, without any intermingled fear of what would chance if they did not ?

By far the greater number must confess that they simply do not know how to set about praying rightly. Prayer with them is dull and ineffectual. They continue willingly enough to pray, but they sometimes ask themselves if there is any sense in praying, and if it were not better to give it up entirely. The contact which they have with the divine world is weak. And sometimes it seems to them that they are scarcely honest with themselves. A university professor of theology, who was strictly orthodox, once said to me, almost in tears, that he had always wished to be able to pray as his mother had prayed—but he left me in no doubt that he felt himself very far from that goal. And when people pray together, as in saying grace or in church, it does not require much sensitiveness of feeling to notice how much of it is done mechanically while the thoughts are entirely elsewhere. If one could hold an investigation into the prayer of men of our time, one would see *how rapid is its decline*. Quite apart from the egoism and all the superstition which creep into men's prayers, the powers of the soul out of which alone men can pray still exist only in a terrifyingly small amount.

When it is told of Christ that He lifted His eyes to heaven, He looked up to His Father, it must have been as if a soul's pure mirror was turned towards the heaven of stars, which mirrored itself brightly in it with great peace. The Gospels give us this impression very strongly, for example in the high-priestly prayer, John xvii. When *we* turn our souls towards heaven, they are like mirrors which have become dull and blind, where, perhaps, a feeble reflection shows ; but no starry heaven.

Thirty years ago, as a young theologian, I tried to find out what occurs in the souls of men when the word "God"

35

is spoken. The result gave sufficient cause for thought. Only a quite common-place turning to the world above could be observed—an unilluminated longing and feeling for it. In the theology of to-day, which knows only a God who is mysterious and afar off, this fact is becoming apparent.

In this need of to-day, the need of an age which has learned to look outwards and down, and thereby forgotten how to look upwards and within, it is in many respects only meditation which can bring help. First of all, we shall learn again by meditation how to represent to ourselves that which is spiritual. We shall learn it slowly, but in a quite honest way. In every meditation, we practise taking something spiritual into our soul, and pondering it. That will, as a matter of course, be beneficial to prayer also. For is it such a bad form of prayer to do nothing for once, but look steadfastly at the divine ? Instead of asking, which we often do, heedlessly, we learn to be silent and look. Thus we are on the way to worship, which our race has lost. It always seems to me that the first three petitions of the Lord's Prayer are meant to lead us upon such a way, and that we ought first of all to seek really to behold and to perceive that of which they speak : the divine name, the divine kingdom, the divine will. In the instruction of candidates for confirmation, and in preaching, one is fond of calling prayer the converse of the soul with God. But that which we would not permit ourselves to do when talking to anyone of high position, we do in this case ; we do not wait until we are spoken to, we bring forward our own wishes and requests, we go fully into everything, and when we have said our say, we go hurriedly away without asking if the other has not also something to say. Many prayers would at once be answered if we could only once really look at God.

Meditation leads to a much purer kind of prayer than that which is usual. It allows God to speak. It teaches us to hear, and so it leads to the "hearing of prayer," which is quite a different thing from the prompt granting of our desires. It teaches us to become aware of the Divine Being, and from it really to receive the divine will for our life. That is a more worthy way of having intercourse with God, and a much more effectual way than when we think that He must be immediately at our service to do our will. Of course, direct help comes from our asking in all times of need. And he who knows how to ask aright will sometimes feel absolutely afraid when he sees how near help was, and how he is surrounded by the heavenly servants of Christ at every moment in which he understands how to call them. But more important than that we ourselves should be helped, is this, that we should grow into the divine will. And meditation is of service to us in this.

But the last and greatest help is that it changes us wholly into petition. That is not saying too much. The more we learn to meditate, so much the more does our soul assume an attitude of petitioning and expectation. The highest meditation is the highest petitioning. Without understanding this one cannot meditate upon a safe and high level. We learn to open ourselves more and more. We learn with a longing which we did not know before, which is itself a prayer, to look towards the divine world; we learn to change ourselves inwardly into a prayer, not that we may attain the fulfilment of any particular wishes, but that we may ourselves become the vessels of divine "fulfilment." It seems to me as if Christ had desired this of His disciples.

When we read His farewell talk, it occurs to us again and again how strangely and impressively He speaks of asking in His name. The picture of the disciples as he wished them to be is one of men who shall do outwardly much greater deeds, who shall show forth "greater works" in the world than He Himself, who shall lead their lives in mighty accomplishment of divine acts : but at the same time inwardly they are much more mighty in their continual petitioning. Their whole inner life is intended to be a perpetual asking from above, petitioning from above, receiving from above. One has the impression that Christ has imagined this inward power of receiving from above as being so great that we can scarcely divine it. To do mighty works outwardly, inwardly to receive the spirit—this is the mark of the true disciple.

The saying, " Ask in My Name," which occurs so often and so urgently in the farewell talk, and which is usually so little and so externally practised, is translated in the Act of Consecration of Man : " May Christ live in our praying."

The meditation which we are here describing, leads to this, that first of all *Christ* can really be present with us ; and then that Christ begins really to live in us. And if He begins to live in us, then no other thing can happen than that He also begins to *pray* in us. For this is His true life within. And then we understand in a new and clear and living way, what it means to pray in Christ's name. It is the highest happiness of man to experience something of this praying of Christ within us—it is a divine happiness. The Act of Consecration of Man brings us to those heights, when it leads us after the transubstantiation to pray Our Father. Quite of itself it makes it easy for us to let Christ pray within us. With the words which He Himself once spoke, and which, at their request, He gave to the disciples as a prayer, He begins His most intimate life within us, and thus passes into us.

But we must reply to those who come to us with the complaint that they have made many attempts to meditate and yet have made no progress. In their impatience people always expect much more rapid progress than is at all possible. We cannot fly up on to the mountains, we can only go slowly step by step. In my case it happened that after a year of straining to meditate I detected scarcely any progress. Then when I came to Dr. Steiner he immediately began to speak of progress; and when I began to express a different opinion he said : " You have made great progress, but you are not yet conscious of it." And so I have accustomed myself, not to be always measuring my progress, but to think of the plants, and I have always reminded others, who were dissatisfied with themselves, of the plants. One cannot be always digging in a flower-pot to see if the seed has grown ; that would be the surest way to kill the plant. One must see that it has light, air and water, and then be able to wait. Even when a plant is already visible in a flower-pot, it often looks for a long time as if it were making no progress. A growing child also often seems for a long time not to be growing, although it is well-fed every day. Then suddenly a month comes in which it shoots up ; it is exactly the same in the inner life. We must have for our inner life, if it is to prosper, the same mood of trust which we bring to the plant and the growing child. If we are dissatisfied, we must see to the air and water, but must not touch the growing seed. It will surely grow of itself if it has the right food.

For a long time the first and only thing that comes is the feeling that one is upon a good way. But sometimes not even that comes. Perhaps a kind of hungry feeling comes if we leave off our inward working at ourselves. There is something remarkable about this hunger of the soul. Usually it comes on, if we regularly cultivate our

39

inner life, exactly at the hour when we have accustomed ourselves to meditate. Like an awakener, it recalls to us our duty. People who are obliged to travel much, and who are thereby thrown out of the regularity of their lives again and again, suffer very much from this lack of rhythm. The feeling is as if one were completely thrown into confusion. In this we can already discover something of the meaning of that which spiritual science calls the etheric body or the vital body. This lowest part of the being of our soul lives strongly in time and rhythm. Therefore rhythm is so beneficial in meditation as well as in ritual. But besides this benefit, rhythm means also a strengthening of one's power; one learns this little by little. In the revolving stream of time, life ever brings back to us that which we last wrought inwardly, and we can then begin there, where we left off. Every right meditation, every deeply experienced Act of Consecration of Man, every Lord's Prayer strongly prayed, brings its own blessing when we turn to it the next time. It then seems as if friendly hobgoblins had built up the house a little further in the time between.

Still worse off than those who do not feel that they are making progress, are those who cannot succeed in meditating at all. One often hears sad complaints that someone has for years tried vainly to meditate. The cultus may be for many people a way by which they may also come to meditate. By the pictures and words which one calls to remembrance again in one's daily work, the service will awaken and train in the right way the mood of reverent, loving self-immersion. Of course the cultus is not simply meant for such people as do not or cannot meditate. Each word which is derogatory to the cultus is keenly felt, by those who know what a ritual really is, to be a sin against a solemn divine reality. In the Christian cultus Christ is present, and is dealing with men. All selfish wishes are dumb in the presence of the sublime act which is being performed. But it is the characteristic and truly Christian mark of the cultus, that it comes down to those also who are not able to meditate actively themselves. It helps those, as it helps others also in another way. Let each one see what most helps him forward, and that is best for him. And then there can be no dispute.

But it can also be said that the honest attempt to meditate, repeated unweariedly, already leads one forward, even when one must ever admit one's powerlessness and lack of skill. I must admit that I know of exercises which I have attempted a thousand times throughout a whole decade, and yet have never been able to complete. Just this calm, consecutive endeavour, even when it does not succeed, may have high spiritual and moral value. But in many cases it happens that one has no idea of what actually occurs. For example, many people complain that they cannot attain to a living feeling of tranquillity. That is really because for the first time they discover how poor and weak their feelings generally are. In their life up to now in which one feeling has trod upon the heels of another—and the feelings have always been reflected by the outward world, and so have seemed greater than they were—they did not become conscious of the fact. And it is the same when a man complains that he cannot hold fast a spiritual content. It is an advance when he begins to notice how feebly until now his thoughts have flickered like a will-o'-the-wisp. Michael Bauer, to whom I owe many very helpful inspirations to meditation, once told me of an acquaintance who said to him : " As soon as I sit down to meditate, it is as if I had upset a bee-hive and all the bees had flown out ; my thoughts flutter about like that." The bee-hive had always been there, and the bees also, but not the man who saw them : he had first awakened in meditation.

But if we wish to proceed in building up the content of our meditations, it would be well if in the background we kept a firm hold upon the two great fundamental meditations for day and night :—I am Love ! and, I am Peace ! He to whom Christ is not yet a living reality may think of God or of the ideal man. From these fundamental meditations let us now go on to become more at home in the " I " which is speaking.

It would indeed be of very great significance if we could come to feel directly this " I " which is speaking. That would be the very greatest gain for a man's life. One may prepare oneself for it by trying to feel other " I's." For example, read a few lines of Goethe, put the book aside and ask yourself what kind of a man, what kind of an " I " has there revealed itself to me ? so one would look into a being whose spirit was light and free and open to the world. One can always find refreshing food in such an " I " without distinguishing any particular perceptions or feelings. As a contrast, one may then read a page of Nietzsche and look closely at this spirit or rather this " I." One then looks into an unusually distinguished, finely-developed " I " which scorns liberty. Such experiments are seldom made by men to-day; but they open up great depths of human spiritual history.

After such preparation, it may be an unique experience to look at the " I " which speaks in John's Gospel. Its purity is that of pure light. It has a sure force which contains in itself no violence, a freedom which radiates sincerity yet contains no licence, and endless power of giving, in which is no weakness. When a man's senses are awake to this, he knows of nothing higher than simply to gaze into this " I " and take a " sun-bath " in it. It is still more, it is a baptism of purification, a Lord's Supper

42

which ever endures. In this, one can hold fast to history. One understands so well the evangelist John, who also desires simply to gaze into this light and who, after he had heard this word " I " in Christ's mouth, does not like to use it for himself—he calls himself only " the disciple whom the Lord loved." But what does one learn of these central miracles from the usual interpretation of John's Gospel? For most men it is certainly not possible without further preparation to gaze into the light of this " I." They may therefore be pleased with the following description of how one may be absorbed in one "I am" after another, and look at the most intimate thing which we are able to perceive—Christ's being.

The first saying is : " I am the Bread of Life " (John vi, 35 and 48).

Through this saying we can perceive the importance which the great religious pictures of the past may have in the training of our inward life. We think of Leonardo's " Last Supper." It is not only a beautiful artistic idea, it is a real revelation to see how in the painting, Christ, with His left hand opened in a gesture of giving, is pushing the bread across the table. If we take this into ourselves, then, in depths of our soul which we ourselves cannot fathom, a mode of being forms itself which is like to that of Christ. Through the picture Christ works sacramentally upon us. He lets His powers pass over to us and dispenses to us a communion. This leads us to ask whether the powers of the adversary also do not often use means, which like the above, act within the unconscious and unperceived, in order to destroy men unawares. Fighting against Christ, in Leonardo's picture, we see Judas, not opening his hand which is nearest Christ's outstretched hand, but clenching it tightly, clutching not bread but stone, the rigid metal. These are the outward hands. But the inward hands also speak with one another and fight with one another in different ways. Two different spirits call to us to make our choice and decision.

Stone and bread—this opposition of these two echoes significantly again and again from the background of the Gospel. When the tempter said to Christ: " If Thou be the Son of God command that these stones be made bread." Christ answered him, " Man shall not live by bread alone, but by every word that proceedeth out of the mouth of God." We ourselves shall learn that temptations overcome always bring corresponding manifestations of grace. Because Christ when tempted spoke these words and lived in accordance with them, he can afterwards, upon the Mount of the Feeding, give to men something higher than bread. He Himself is " the word that proceedeth out of the mouth of God," by which man can live. " Man cannot live by bread alone " ; that reechoes sublimely from Heaven as Christ passes along the rows of men and feeds them out of His divine life.

And so we come near to the meaning which the pictures in the Gospels themselves have for meditation. We must, especially in the pictures of John's Gospel, look through the outward happening into the history of the world itself. It is humanity which is resting there upon the mountain. Christ goes with all His living power through the ranks. His disciples are significant only as His helpers. From Christ the power goes forth which feeds men. The great feeling of the giving of thanks spreads itself over the picture and penetrates all in a wonderful way.

If we are able so to receive Himself and so to experience His words that we can say with the Act of Consecration of Man, " Through Thy word my soul becomes whole,"—if we are able out of our own experience to assent to the confession of Peter, " Lord to whom shall we go? Thou hast the words of eternal life," then we are upon the path on which the saying about the bread of life is fulfilled.

In this way we may learn to enter into Christ and to feed upon Him. For He has come to feed us. The first "I am" tells us that. It leads us into a more vital Christianity than is commonly to be found. When we strengthen our experience by observing how the lives of good and great men can feed and nourish us, how there is an innermost part of us which lives solely by such food, the meaning of Christ for our lives will become ever greater and more powerful. He is really *the food*. Our very inmost part lives *only* from Him. This part remains always hungry if it is not fed by Him.

We now begin to understand clearly many sayings of the Gospel about those who hunger. One may even receive the impression that that in us which lives from Christ becomes ever more important, and that which lives from " bread alone " ever more unessential. The people who fasted in order to be better able to devote themselves to Christ guessed this secret. And tales are even told of saints who lived only on the host. They are a prophecy.

The sacrament of the altar also is shown to us in a new light. It prepares us for a new kind of feeding. In Paradise there stood a tree of which it was said :—" In the day that thou eatest thereof thou shalt surely die." Now there stands upon earth a tree of which it is true that " in the day that thou eatest thereof thou shalt learn what life means." And the whole of the sixth chapter of John's Gospel, which contains the saying about the bread of life, is filled with such harmonies culminating in the music of the resurrection. " I will raise him up at the last day ! " It is just this resurrection experience of the bread of life that one would wish for man. When we can once enter into Christ and feed on Him in the higher sense, we shall first truly learn what food is and nourishment, what life is and resurrection. Christ is *the* bread.

When we thus begin to learn to know the inward feeding, then we shall soon notice how the outward feeding becomes for us something different. The bodily process becomes transparent for a happening which becomes always more spiritual. We learn ever more sacramentally that here is something which gives itself to us and offers itself for us. We hear ever more clearly an " I " in the bread which lies upon the table. We see ever more reverently the same process going on in the daily food, and in what occurred when Christ offered Himself upon the cross for us. It is the same " I " which says both here and there, " I am the Bread." This is much more than Luther said, when he spoke of the " dear daily bread." Luther spoke out of his warm-hearted nature, but here we gaze into a sublime world of spiritual revelation. The same God who led Christ to sacrifice Himself upon the cross speaks to us from every piece of bread which offers its divine sacrifice upon our table. The grace at table gains another meaning. We understand why eating for men of past ages was connected with the cult. And we shall soon find that our eating is redeemed from a terrible barbarism if even a breath of this feeling is mingled with it. Yes, we shall even observe that our food feeds us in quite a different way when we thus receive and enjoy it with giving of thanks.

But from the bread there now goes out a process which lays hold of the rest of the world also. Through our " enjoyment " of the food upon the table, the word " enjoy " becomes different for us. We begin to feel that we are at a divine table. We begin to return into Paradise ; ye *shall* eat of all the trees of the garden ! The

46

flowers become for us, not only a joy, but really a food, and so do the stars. The bread of life is in the sunbeams which come to us, and also in the majesty of the mountains. This is only touched upon. Let only one thing be pointed out. The tempter once asked Christ to turn stones into bread. When we get so far as to be able to see the great rocky mountains spiritually, and eat them like bread, then Christ has wrought that miracle in us. He has changed stones into bread, but conversely, His adherents often did the opposite and changed the bread of life into stone.

Men often speak to-day of their view of the world. But they do not know that they cannot simply read up a view of the world, or think it out, but must work it out with the whole self. This will be revealed ever more clearly in the future. Men stare into the world like children. But they do not know that there is also an inner training of one's ordinary sight, and that the world itself then looks quite different. On the other hand this work at one's own spiritual nature will take the place of the earlier believing acceptance of dogma. More active, more " dynamic " as people like to say to-day, will one's view of the world as well as one's faith become. One will not simply be able to take over Christianity as a systematic organism of thought, but one will be obliged personally to work it out inwardly, step by step, as a new world, as a quite new spirituality in the Holy Ghost, who comes to us through Christ.

The Christian picture of the world is the great Last Supper. In all things around us we hear the divine word in an ever more living way. And this divine word makes itself known to us as the same word which became flesh in Christ. But this word does not speak to us, it feeds us. Everywhere, deep within us we hear the same voice :— " I am the Bread of Life." We are at the Lord's Table.

Christ and Judas are opposite to one another. All this *cannot* be achieved without hard work of our own. Christ says in the 27th verse of this 6th chapter of John's Gospel: " Labour not for the meat which perisheth, but for that meat which endureth unto everlasting life, which the Son of Man shall give unto you." What does it mean when it says that we ourselves must labour for the food which is to feed us ? And when Christ then continues : " for him hath God the Father sealed," we may say that in meditation we unseal this seal.

We must, therefore, through this meditation gradually come to penetrating Christ until He is still only bread, and then penetrating this bread until it is only Christ. Then this meditation will unfold its full meaning for our view of the world, as well as for our daily life.

But it is necessary to raise this task, which is set us, as much as possible above what is narrow and personal, and to see it in its greatness, in its relation to the cosmos. In the *west*, Mankind has thought only of the word "bread." One "earns one's daily bread." One struggles for " daily bread." But that is not the "bread of life." And indeed, the outward bread is beginning to lose its food value through the artificial manures which are meant to increase it. It is becoming dead. In the *east*, on the contrary, humanity has concentrated upon a life which is above the earth, which is losing its relation to daily bread and its duty, a life which they often seek also to reach through fasting—while over the earth, which they have not taken seriously enough, famine breaks out as is constantly happening in India and China. Christ leads us into a life which is bread: and to a bread which is life. He calls us to a royal banquet. We shall understand, in an ever more living way, that the church service which is most Christlike, is not that in which one merely hears the word of Christ, as in the Protestant service, but the Christlike service is that in which Christ is the meal—still more immediately than can ever happen in words. Because Christ is the bread, He is proclaimed to us through a meal. The Act of Consecration of Man also is not intended only to be heard and to be celebrated, but in all its details to be received as a food for the soul.

If in this saying "I am the Bread of life," we have looked down, in the second "I am" we look up. "I am the Light of the world" (John viii, 12). And with this word also we must change our accustomed world. Just this spiritual working upon the *world* is necessary if *man* is to become new. Just this saying of Christ about light can gradually become for us a real temple in which we spend our time with great joy. So as to get out again of the narrow personal Christianity into a Christianity as great as the world, we may remember in spirit all those who have ever worshipped in the temples of light. In silent vanished centuries our brother men have sent up their souls in prayer to the light. We think of the old holy Rishis, how they through long ages taught their pupils to pray: "We would receive into us the love-awaking light of the great sun-being, which gives life, that it may help our spirit onwards." We think of royal Zarathustra, how he brought to his Persians reverence of the spirit-ruling majesty of the golden sun. We hear the sacred song of the sun echoing from the Egyptian temples in Thebes, in Memphis, in Heliopolis.

We may also think of later times : of how, in the Middle Ages, Francis walked under the glowing sun of Italy :

Praised be Thou, O Lord, with all Thy creatures,
    And especially our brother the sun,
He makes the day, and we are lighted by him,
    And he is beautiful, and shines with great
      splendour,
And of Thee O most high he is the symbol.

Of how in misty Holland, Rembrandt, hungry for light, conceived of his whole art as a feeling after the wonders of light, as a priest's service of light, of how, at the summit of German history, Goethe reverently gazed into the "deeds and sorrows of light," of how, in the colours, he recognised the revelation of the Elohim, of how, in his last confession, he reverenced the sun, along with Christ, as the most mighty divine revelation, "which it is granted to us men on earth to see."

All this we may bring to mind within us. Then we may think of the first divine word of the Bible: "Let there be light," and of the last one about the new world to come: "They need no candle, neither light of the sun for the Lord God giveth them light." (Rev. xxii, 5.) Between these two words let us place the word of Christ, "I am the Light of the world," a new "Let there be light." But let it come from within that it may shine through all that is outward. To-day many meditations are given and carried out, which are concerned with light. It is in the deepest sense wholesome and it brings deliverance if we seek through Christ's being till we experience Him only as light, and penetrate this light until it is Christ Himself. We can best do this, if we allow ourselves to be guided by the seven great acts of Christ upon earth, as recorded in John's Gospel. They are like a working of light in a higher sphere.

First let us represent the outward light before us in spirit, as a sea of waves of life, and let us dive deep into this light as into a healing spring. We feel how our whole being breathes in health in the light. We feel how powers of healing stream forth from the light. And let us seek to experience Christ in this way. Let us think not only of His words, but let us think that the power of healing proceeds from His words, as when the woman became whole by touching the hem of His garment, or the son of the nobleman was healed from a distance. (John iv, 51.) Then let us seek to experience how the light has something still more inward to give our souls, how they must be pure, if they are to live in light, how purity flows forth from the worlds of light. This purifying power of light lives in unimagined fullness in Christ. " Ye are clean through the word which I have spoken unto you," says Christ to His disciples. That is the healing of sins in the light of Christ. (John xv, 3.) Then let us seek to listen to the divine harmonies of light, to the deep tranquillity and contentment which makes us part of the divine working. And let us look from there to Christ as He says, " The peace be with you." The gates of Paradise open through His words, and the harmonies of heaven spread themselves around. So may the disciples have been encouraged when He met them upon the water : " It is I, be not afraid." (John vi, 20.) Then let us seek to become wholly light in this light. As in the sunlight, when we give ourselves to it, we seem to become light, through and through, as if we should think in sunbeams, so let us seek to fill ourselves from Christ with divine light in every corner of our being. Let us seek to illuminate with Christ, the Light, first, our own being, then the world in which we live, then the great world beyond. We are one light with Him. We seek to perceive in this light ; even if it is only a vague perception. Christ makes the blind see. (John ix, 39.) But a food also comes from the sunlight. It is as if a starving man within us had waited for this food of light, as if he wanted to eat his fill at the table of light. And so the light of Christ is for the light within us " the bread that comes down from heaven and gives life to the world." (John vi, 33.) Again a great power that can change the world lives in the light, as if with the light the whole world of creation would enter into us, as if we could not remain as we are if we gave ourselves up to the power of this light. So also is Christ's being. Every word from Him moulds us anew. In each word of His there is plenary power, as in the beginning of the world. In each word of His lies sleeping the new man, to which we shall awake after God's likeness. So Christ " reveals His glory " as at the marriage of Cana. (John ii, 11.) Now we have reached the last and greatest. In the light there is Easter, a morning song of joy sung by all spirits, a " day of the Lord " which will break in us also. And in the saying of Christ the resurrection is present with power. He stands ever before us and rolls away the stone from the grave's mouth : " Lazarus, come forth ! " (John xi, 43.) The radiance of day has come. It is called : " Christ."

All these are only suggestions. They lead us upon a sure path into the world of the " I " which is light, in which the daily sunlight and the highest divine revelation are one in Christ. This is the act of serving God in the temple of the sun.

Again we may turn our glance to the east and to the west. In the west men have achieved their ego. But there is no light in this ego. In the east men have honoured the light. But they have not found their ego in the light. But we are going towards a new world, where we with Christ shall " shine as the same light." " Then shall the righteous shine as the sun in the kingdom of the Father." As Christ says of Himself, " I am the Light of the world ! " so would He say of His disciples, " Ye are the Light of the world ! "

IV

A YOUNG girl once explained to me how difficult it
was for her at home to get any time, even if it were
only ten minutes, in which she might quietly occupy herself with herself. If she withdrew to her room, immediately someone knocked at the door: "What are you doing
in there? Have you nothing to do?" Christians are not
allowed by their "fellow Christians" to carry out Christ's
advice : "When thou prayest, go into thy chamber and
shut thy door." To most men a prayer in the day-time,
apart from a grace said at table, would appear to be extraordinary, probably even a piece of idleness. Many
people who wish to meditate, especially women and young
people who are growing up, simply do not know how to
make it possible to be alone in their own homes. As
regards our inward life we are still living in a state of un-
heeding barbarism. The fundamental right of a man to
be quite alone by himself, in order that afterwards he may
be more to other men, is far from being recognised to be a
matter of course. In this state of affairs nothing but a
tenacious struggle, which must be carried on in the most
friendly yet unyielding way, even in the face of de-
liberate obstruction and derision, can be of any use.
We shall choose the suitable time and opportunity, and
shall withdraw for inward quiet, attracting as little as
possible the notice and the attack of other people. But
we must clearly recognise that it is usually the bad conscience of the other people which is the real adversary.
The others feel that one is right and that they ought to do
it also. If one perceives this one will go one's way more
peacefully.

Women have often said to me that their first opportunity of a free quarter-of-an-hour in the morning comes
after the husband has gone to business, and the children to
school. But then they must beware lest the cares of the
household break into their spiritual temple. Others
find no chance until evening. Then arises the danger that
weariness will overcome us, or sleep. I have been able
to help many with this advice, that they could at least
begin their meditation immediately after a meal, when
the digestive system begins its work, and rest five or ten
minutes with closed eyes, but quite awake, perhaps lying
down, so that they may have strength for inward activity.
For many it is easiest to turn to meditation immediately
after awaking in the morning, while they are still lying
down, and perhaps have not yet opened their eyes. One
must sometimes secure this morning meditation with
some trouble. But it is very good and effective, thus to
pass from sleep into one's spiritual temple and dwell
there before one begins the day.

But personal and household relationships are so different that it is almost impossible to give general advice.
Only this can be said with great emphasis to everyone who
seeks to cultivate his inner life :—" Fight to secure the
quiet quarter-of-an-hour, under all circumstances, if
possible morning *and* evening, and if it is possible (we
shall speak later of the reason why it is important) also at
mid-day. Our higher self is at stake. The time which we
withdraw from our work and from those who belong to
us, comes richly back in the quality of our being. And if
we shorten our time for rest by this quarter-of-an-hour,
we need not worry. As necessary as the daily bread, yes,
even more necessary are these free times, and they
ought, like eating, to be a matter of course in our lives.

We shall soon find out that the actual opponents of our
meditation are to be looked for not among the other

members of our household, not in outward circumstances, however difficult our household circumstances may be, but in ourselves. It is true that the housewife can with difficulty repress the restless business which makes her remember all the possible things which must be done at once, and the man whose profession causes anxiety also finds it difficult to do this, although they both well understand that everything can well wait a quarter-of-an-hour. But when we are obliged to say to ourselves in the evening, " to-day again we did not succeed in finding time for meditation," and when we try to excuse ourselves, " this time it was impossible, absolutely impossible," then if we think it over carefully, we shall usually find that we ourselves were not really willing. We ourselves have always put something else forward which was supposedly a hindrance, but was really a self-made excuse. And so we first notice how much cunning insincerity we possess within, which always seduces us from our higher duties ; how unwilling a man is to follow his own will, as soon as anything of the divine will enters into this will. He does not want to exert himself, but wishes to have everything through " Grace." And so, again, we first notice how many objections to " self-redemption " through meditation, which are alleged to come from a " belief in God's grace," are nothing else but the unwillingness of man to go one step to meet the grace offered to him, or even to open his hand to receive the gift presented to him. For all that we here describe is nothing but opening of the hand to take the divine gift offered to us. Behind the most pious upward glance an evil may dwell, which will not suffer the true God to enter into us. If we have once discovered in us the evil habit of wilfulness, which would cheat us of meditation, as it would cheat us of any earnest inward exertion of our wills, and if we begin to keep strict watch on it and to pass over nothing, then we have taken an important step in our inward life. Truly the adversary of meditation is *in* us, and really never outside us.

We shall notice this especially in the hours when we set about paying more attention to ourselves, and examining and changing the content of our souls, in those hours when we formerly allowed our thoughts and feelings to flutter about aimlessly. A woman, when she is busy with her household affairs has an especially good opportunity of " Pondering in her heart " this thing or that. And one's real being is formed by it. A man has similar opportunities when his work is mechanical, or when going to and returning from his place of business, or when he has a pause, or has a wearisome journey to go. It is of great importance to come gradually to control all the times when we formerly let ourselves go and dreamed. But we shall see—this may be observed especially when we are going to sleep—with how much headstrong insistence our thoughts go their own way, and defend themselves against any kind of control. If we then look back at what has been occupying us for perhaps a quarter-of-an-hour, we shall find that it is not worthy to be entertained in our soul. But with stubborness, as if for dear life, our souls insist upon going their own ways, whether after little pleasures and fancies with which we enjoy ourselves, or after all kinds of vexations and resentments, with which also we obviously enjoy ourselves just as much, for we cannot get free from them. It really is a matter of death, the death of the old man in us. The more we succeed in ennobling our unconscious and involuntary life, in spiritualising it, in making it Christlike, the greater heights shall we attain in our conscious and free life. What is best will come forth at the right moment from a soul which, in the freest play of its thinking and feeling, has a great and good content which feeds and forms it.

56

The " I ams " help us to a new view of the world, at which we must work, not only in our solitary thinking, but in our daily lives. In the saying : " I am the Bread of Life," we look down. In it we discover that which gives, which sacrifices, in the world beneath us. And thus we look into the face of the person of the Father who speaks through Christ. The bread is the messenger and the spokesman of this kingdom. But its word is true for all which is under us, even for the stone and for the animal. In the saying, " I am the Light of the World," we look upward. The light is the representative of the higher kingdoms. As the world below us feeds us, so the world above us gives us light. The light makes known to us everything which happens to our spirits, when we draw near to the higher worlds. Spiritual light fills us from above. And through the light appears to us again the face of the person of the Father, who speaks in Christ. The third " I am," " I am the Door " (John x, 7) leads our glance outward to the people around us. And the fourth " I am," " I am the Good Shepherd," will then lead us within, to the inward guiding.

In Christianity it is a matter of course that one should pray for others. Christ prayed for His own, and, especially in the High Priestly prayer, has allowed us to look deep into the matter of His prayer for the disciples. One can never learn from it enough of the way in which, quite without illusion, and yet with inward sympathy, He brings His disciples before the Father. One becomes ever more thankful that there is this prayer, whose benediction Christians are still far from realising. The Apostle Paul also prayed for his churches. What he says in his letters, and the manner in which he says it, would not have been possible had not the very soul of his apostolic work been a similar strong praying for his churches. The intercourse of men would be inspired quite differently, inspired by a breath from a higher world, if we knew how to take our contemporaries rightly into the divine light. We must first lose in this divine light all the short-sighted selfishness which we harbour in respect of them. And this may be the first effect of such new prayer.

To such new prayer this third "I am," "I am the Door," may lead us. Then the question which one often hears, "Is intercession of any use?" would answer itself. Does not God Himself know what is good for the others? Ought He at my feeble prayer to do anything which He would not Himself have done, or to leave undone anything which He would otherwise have done? We should like to oppose this with a mighty fact in the opposite sense. Often in life one receives the impression, "If this person had been prayed for, rightly and earnestly, he would not have come to this." One feels that angels are looking down and asking, "Are there people who are praying for him? Then we can do much that otherwise is impossible." Prayers rise as spiritual power to the divine world. There, humanly speaking, they alter the whole state of the case. They create new spiritual possibilities for the divine guiding powers, quite apart from the fact that they act directly upon him for whom prayer is offered, especially when he is aware, but also when he is not aware of it, because they fill the whole spiritual atmosphere around him with good thoughts and impulses, which can inspire him, even when he thinks they are only chance ideas of his own. Many people have felt very clearly, especially in sickness and at the time of death, that they are being prayed for. But quite apart from all this, such prayers are in the higher world, to use an illustration, like new living threads, which the angels can weave with their own into the web of fate, and for which they often wait. Thus man becomes a fellow-worker upon the fate of his fellow-men, within modest limits certainly, but one cannot yet trust him beyond that. But, even counting the fact that through prayer from beneath the powers and possibilities of the spiritual world are made richer, we cannot form a lively enough or free enough conception of the intercourse of men with the divine world. The higher world listens to man, it pays attention to him, it takes him seriously. Often, certainly, his prayer cannot be answered, because it would be harmful to him if it were, and because in the higher world one lives in the light of a wisdom into which a human being cannot penetrate. But we need only read through the farewell talks of Christ, and the ever-repeated invitations to pray in His name which occur in them, and one will know that Christ wishes to have with men such intercourse as " when a man speaks with his friend," to apply the wonderful phrase about the conversation of Jehovah with Moses. He expects that man should know with whom he speaks, but He is also ready to enter into the man who is united to Him, and share his fate with him. Everyone who has even the slightest idea of prayer as Christ thought of it, knows that the heavenly helpers of Christ are, when they are called, so quickly at hand and so near to us, that one almost trembles, and is sacredly afraid of summoning them too lightly, and also, that one is surrounded by them as by a heavenly host, and that they do all that can possibly be done.

What this saying, "I am the Door," is capable of meaning I learned decades ago, when I myself had not yet thought much about it. I then sought, as a teacher of religion, some help to thought which would put me in the right mood when I went into the school. Then there occurred to me the saying of Christ in His high-priestly prayer, " Thine they were, and Thou gavest them me and I have manifested Thy name unto them." I represented to myself that this saying should be the actual door through which alone I dared to go to my children. I put away all thought of the physical door. " Thine they are and Thou gavest them Me, and I must manifest Thy name unto them "—through this, as through an invisible spiritual door, ought I to go my way to the children. So this word has been of extraordinarily great service to me, and it would have been of still greater service had I had the courage and the strength to take it more earnestly. One can indeed regard such a saying as the door through which one goes to the sick, the prisoners, or the poor. Then we shall come in quite a different way to the realisation of such a saying of Christ as this : " I was sick and ye visited me not." Such sayings would hover above one like an invisible spiritual world.

In these studies we are trying, not only to become familiar with the different sayings of Christ, but also in different ways to make them our own. This saying about the door is specially suitable for those who wish to be leaders of men, and it has many sides which we are leaving in the background. But one is acting in the spirit of Christ and the higher life when one makes Christ the door through which one goes in thought to other men. It is as if one placed a sphere of purest selflessness between oneself and the other, and permitted oneself only through this sphere to go to him, to speak to him, and especially, to think of him. Truly, we ought to accustom ourselves not to think of him so outwardly, but only through this pure sphere. Soon we shall have a deep understanding for the saying of Christ which Christ speaks at this very point : " All who do not go through this door are thieves and robbers." We shall more and more appear to ourselves to be really intruders when we think with selfish wishes and interests of others.

The intercourse of men with one another is still very

primitive and troubling to the soul. A few polite
customs do not help us. In no way can we work to
ennoble human intercourse better than by taking this
saying, "I am the Door," seriously. It will first begin to
give us of its inexhaustible blessing if, in our quiet hours,
we regularly meditate with the help of this saying upon
our fellow men, even upon those nearest to us. We
place them before us in the spirit and do not permit ourselves to go to them through any other door than Christ.
Then we become aware, not only of heights of intercourse of which till then we have known nothing, but we
begin for the first time to see our fellow-men and our
"neighbours." We do not interfere egotistically with
their inner life, but allow them to live, just as they are, in
our thoughts. And so we begin to rejoice in them, as
they are, in their actual beings, in spite of their faults.
We become thankful just because they are there. And
this thankfulness that the other is there, is the atmosphere in which he can best thrive, feels himself most at
ease, and can best make progress. We feel deeply the
best in the other, the God's thought which hovers over
him, the " Glory " which he has " in God," and can thus
unite ourselves to this his true ego. Intercourse with
men acquires a solemn radiance of which we have known
nothing before.

We know that in the marriage ritual of the Christian
Community the " gate of community of life " is
mentioned, and that in the course of the marriage service
the rings pass from one to the other over the picture of
Christ. In this a high ideal of marriage stands before us :
that the wedded pair go to one another through Christ as
the door, in every thought and feeling if possible. This
also must be practised in our quiet hours. So will this
saying, "Thine they are", become ever more living for us.

But in this way one will find out that one must enlarge

the sphere of selflessness still more. To be selfless is not to be without an ego. He alone can be selfless who has an ego. Yes, the stronger our own ego is, the more strongly will the ego of the other echo in us, the more will the other ego be in consonance with it; be so in consonance with it that we are united within a higher common Ego. There are many mysterious events in intercourse with men, and this is one of the most wonderful. In every hour in which we have such intercourse with another ego in the sphere of selflessness, we hear this saying: " All are one in me!" Here men are placed before the greatest and most beautiful of all experiences—a real unison in Christ, in comparison with which the most beautiful harmonies and accords of music belong to a lower sphere. The " I am " is the door. Only the ego must sound in us as it has sounded in Christ.

We therefore make the following suggestion for meditation. Let us create between ourselves and others a sphere in which we let unselfishness shine forth like pure light. Let us let this light become the " I am " of Christ. Let us go through this door to those whom we love and to those whom we do not love. Let us look at them as they appear to us if we go through this door. Then that which takes place within us will lead us to a new kind of intercession. We shall learn how many people will " open their hearts " to us, but also how many are closed, because, until now, we have thought about them with curiosity and in a false and hasty way. We shall acquire quite different standards of judgment, shall not speak as formerly of sympathetic and unsympathetic, of strange and hostile, but we shall see the egos in their un-fathomableness and in their connection with one another. We shall begin to understand sayings like those of Master Eckehart : " As long as thou dost allow to thyself more than thou allowest to that stranger whom thou hast never

62

seen, so long hast thou failed to see into the depths of God," or that of Christ, " Thou shalt love thy neighbour as thyself." We shall have with every man an experience like that of Alcibiades with Socrates : " A poor dwelling, but in it lives a God." We shall find that the guardian of the door opens to us, to whom he would not otherwise have opened. We shall come nearer to the goal of humanity in John's Gospel : " I in them, and they in Me, and all one in Me." Gradually will it become sacredly dear to us to go to men through this door, and we shall wish to go then in no other way than through this door.

If, in order to draw in like a breath the greatness of this revelation for the history of the world, we look again towards the East and towards the West, we shall see that in the East men had often this door to others, *Tat twam asi :* " It is thou ! " But the ego was markedly absent. " It is *I*," said Christ, when He said to us, " That which ye have done unto one of the least of these my brethren, ye have done it unto *Me*." And therefore in the East indeed, there comes a feeling of belonging to one another, but in such a way that the souls seek to realise how in their primal source in the godhead they are still one. The fellowship which is pointed to in John's Gospel is quite different. In it men will be made one in the future, but now no longer the souls but the egos are made one. And it is not identity but unity, which can be reached only through Christ. In the West it is quite different. As in the West men live as far apart as possible in their houses, so in life they stand over against one another as individuals. And although one may be enthusiastic for democracy, that is not real community, but the rule of the majority of individuals. The ego has always the tendency to try to impose its own will, and only in order to attain this personal rule does it condescend to bring others over to its own opinion. There is no real door to the other. It is shut, and opens only when the bell rings for some particular purpose. And so we see what we must conquer for the whole of humanity when Christ says to the East, " The door is my ego " and to the West, " My ego is the door."

Now when we have looked below, above and outwards, we are drawn to look inward also, " I am the good shepherd." (John x, 11.) This saying raises especial difficulties for a man of the present time. In the first place, it savours of sentimentality. Secondly, the shepherd's vocation is now far in the past for him, and the lamb is felt to be a picture of helpless imprudence and of patience which puts up with anything, rather than a picture of purity and obedience. It is not easy entirely to get over such feelings and become at home in the feeling which for thousands of years the shepherd has had to his flock, and the animals to their shepherd. The sheep feel their shepherd to be a higher being. And the shepherd gives himself to his sheep, even sacrificing life itself for them. And this brings us to Christ Himself. His ultimate being is clearly expressed when the next sentence after the saying, " I am the good shepherd," says nothing about leading or following, but points to the above fact: "The good shepherd lays down his life for the sheep." A human vocation, which through immeasurable ages has had the greatest significance among humanity, and which, in opposition to the warrior's calling, has embraced the world of peace and prosperity, is here taken up into a higher sphere, and exalted there for ever.

We may now, following the indications given in the parable, try to rise to the worlds of experience in which the secret of inward guidance manifests itself. The first experience is pointed out in the words : " My sheep hear my voice," " I know my sheep and am known of mine." In other New Testament writings also one finds this

64

experience of a deep "knowing." "Then shall I know, even as also I am known." Plato says that all true knowing rests upon a re-knowing of that which the soul already experienced in a higher world before birth.

The kind of knowing which is here spoken of, lies one step higher. The unique love which is aroused in us for Christ, when we once see Him as He is, comes solely because the thought arises in us : There is our true being as it ought to be : there is our divine ego. Man has this experience of Christ at the moment when he sees Him as He really is. But it is good to bring it fully into one's consciousness, and this meditation will serve to do so. We may begin in this way, that we seek to become aware of ourselves in the Light of Christ, as we are meant to be. Then can a " knowing," than which there is none deeper, pass over our soul. Now the divine thought about our being flashes out. Now our real ego shines forth. As when the light of the sun falls upon a diamond which lay dark under other stones and earth, so Christ and our real ego greet one another. They shine as *one* mutual light, like the diamond and the sun. In this picture we may seek to meditate upon the truth : " I know my sheep and am known of mine." This experience may rise to the thought : none but Christ knows me by name : I was hidden, even from myself, until He called me by my name ; but now I know myself, or at least guess what I am, and know that I am known. When I think of Christ, then I think at the same time of my best self, and when I think of my real ego, then Christ in whom it is hidden shines out in me, " To Him the porter openeth." There is really a porter in us who opens only to Christ. We are " closed " until He comes. In every moment in which we really do what is right for us, we do it out of such a deep " knowing."

When one learns this, then there comes an indescribable feeling of safety. One feels that one was in a strange land before, that the shepherd, to quote the parable in Luke's Gospel, has found the lost sheep and is carrying it. One did not know before how far astray one had gone, or how safe one could feel in the world. "They shall never perish, neither shall any man pluck them out of my hand." But this is only so when one obeys the voice of the Leader. Otherwise a feeling of being completely lost sets in. One did not know that one had always lived in this feeling of being lost.

After the feeling of security comes the feeling of safe guidance. This guidance comes entirely from within. We need expect no guidance in signs or beckonings from without, or if there seem to be such, we must enquire carefully into them. The guide lives within. But not for one moment does sure guidance fail when once we are able to distinguish the voice of the guide amid the babel of voices within. Men will learn to listen in quite a different way to the voice of the guide in their soul. Christ has said to us that He will dwell in us. One would choose to go always in the guidance of this leader alone. But it is hard to attain to this. An inward obedience, pure and watchful, will lead us upon a marvellously sure way through life.

The last feeling is the feeling of being rich. We enter worlds of blessing. A sure development begins : "I give unto them eternal life." We know that the true pasture of the soul blossoms there. And all the gardens of the higher worlds open to us.

If, in the previous meditation, we have heard Christ's "I am" before us so that it was the door through which we went, now we may hear it as if it were behind and above us. And it may often be that, when we turn to Him with some important question, if we only have patience to let this " I am " become strong enough, it is as if out of this " I am " we hear the voice which leads us, while it calls us in our true being which it lovingly spares and tends. It is usually only our feeling which prevents us hearing the voice. We are afraid that it may tell us to do what we do not wish to do. This fear often conceals the voice of Christ in us.

In the Eastern world men have sought the " Master," but he was *outside* man. In the Western world men have indeed had the guidance *within*. But no higher ego was there, no divine master who led. Here again in the announcement of Christ in John's Gospel, we have the uniting of the worlds that are falling asunder, and their exaltation by the Christ's gift of the ego. But it is necessary in this meditation to be fully conscious that just here, where He speaks of guidance, Christ is careful to claim His rank as guide only from His power of self-devotion : that on the one side He points to the Father : " I and the Father are one," and on the other side He says just here, of men : " Ye are Gods " (John x, 34). We have not space here to speak of the many details of such a chapter. But we must know, and be always able to bring to life within us, the emotional background out of which Christ's word is spoken.

But the most important thing is this, that it gradually becomes clearer to us how our whole world is now changing. Whenever we look, the divine " I " shines upon us. When we look *down*—the bread is the representative of this kingdom—an "I" looks upon us, who gives His life to us. When we look *up*—the light is the prophet of this world—then again an " I " looks upon us that allows us to share His life. When we look *outwards* we find in our fellow-men the divine radiance, the darkened " I " in the father : and when we look *inwards* again, the great divine " I " stands there, behind us. Everywhere worlds of light arise. But the word "light" is much too thin and lifeless. Out of the light appears everywhere an "I." If we are not to stop short at our first feeling of it, then we must conquer for ourselves this world under us, above us, outside us, in us. And then behind the old world arises a new world, spiritually great and full of love. Wherever we look, we look into the face of a father of whom Christ is the expression of the ego. We begin to feel the far-off greatness of the central saying of the gospel of John: "I in the Father."

V

CHRIST'S walking on this earth must have been a marvellous self-recognition. He looked up to the light, and in the innermost being of light, He found Himself—I am the Light of the world. He looked down to the earth, took up the bread and said again " That, I am." Nothing greater than this recognition had ever happened in a man's soul.

Christ expressed that which He now felt to be His own innermost being in the parable of the good shepherd. In it, without mentioning the word love, He spoke of devotion even unto death. To this corresponds the saying about the door to other men which can only be found in selfless love. According to His own saying, Christ spoke no word " of Himself," but announced " that which the Father had given Him." And so He has revealed to men the " Name of God." In the Old Testament the greatest moment is that in which Jehovah met Moses in the loneliness of the desert, and in answer to the question : " What is thy name ? " replied, " I am the I am ; that is My name ; by it shall I be thought of for ever and ever." This " I am " is taken up by Christ and filled with all its rich content. The name of God is " revealed."

All that we have discussed hitherto is nothing but an exposition of the first request in the Lord's Prayer : " Hallowed be Thy name "—an exposition such as is given by the Gospels. Despite the countless times that the Lord's Prayer has been prayed, this first request has hardly been at all living or concrete to men. They scarcely get beyond a very ordinary feeling of holiness or reverence. Here the way is shown by which life may become the fulfilment of this request, as we become able everywhere, above and below, without and within, to read the name of God and to hallow it. By it man raises himself at the same time to the last and highest knowledge which is possible. All knowledge is ultimately knowledge of God. But knowledge of God is, in the sense of John's Gospel, the true " blessedness." " This is life eternal that they may know Thee, the only true God, and Jesus Christ whom Thou hast sent." And thus all human knowledge becomes deeper and truer the more it becomes like to the self-knowledge of Christ which we have described above.

In our time, when life, belying itself, has set itself strongly to the acquisition of knowledge, it does not help to redeem men to call them away from knowledge to that which, with grand words and confused thinking, one calls " Faith," but it does help to redeem them if one carries knowledge itself onwards, raising it to its Johannine height, which is to-day still the utmost height, a far-off height, above all our present knowledge. For all physical and chemical knowledge, all biological and mathematical-astronomical knowledge leads only to a richer and deeper revelation of the " I am " which lives behind all phenomena. It is therefore the hallowing of the life of thought, of the striving of our present age for knowledge, towards which we are developing through these meditations on the " I ams "—in full harmony with the Gospel.

Up till now we have been looking into a new world of space with its four directions: upward, downward, out-ward, inward. The last three "I ams" help us similarly to build up a new time.*

* Note : incidentally, I hear that there are not seven but eight " I ams."
The saying, " Thou sayest that I am a king " (John xviii, 37) is added ;
but this saying, or rather, this answer belongs, as may be easily seen, to a different order of confession, and along with the answer, " I am the Messiah " (John iv, 26) and the answer " I am the Son of God " (Luke xxii, 70) forms a group of confessions.

At the present time men have a strong feeling for the costliness of time, for its value in money, but little feeling for the holiness of time. For example, they do not know what it means to sit in the sacred stream of time and bathe in it, as the Indians bathe in the Ganges. It was in old Persia that men first became clearly awake to space and time. While the Indians built themselves up and rejoiced and feared in the infiniteness of space and time, we find in Zarathustra sublime words about the god who reveals himself in space and time. We must win back these experiences in a new way. "Weaving in the widths of space and in the depths of time," says the Act of Consecration of Man.

The first thing which we allow to bring us a new future may be the saying; " I am the resurrection and the life " (John xi, 25). In this saying we may once and for all immerse our future, as it were, baptising it in it. Everywhere that future is precious in which Christ's ego arises and guides a new life. All that we see around us is a grave, out of which Christ is willing to arise. The men of to-day have no real future. If they think of the future of the earth, they represent to themselves an endless development to which, however, an end is appointed by the relentless approach of destruction by heat. And concerning themselves, men believe that death may well be the end of all, and that the only brave, honourable and modest thing is to desire no further life ; but if it should continue they hope to be a fair average representative of the majority, if they have behaved themselves fairly decently here upon earth. Now that the old Easter faith has collapsed, men will never come to a new Easter faith except by the help of this saying : " I am the resurrection and the life." They may make all sorts of spiritualistic guesses perhaps. But a belief in what lies beyond this life, which can endure and which in the fullest sense makes life fruitful, must be built up to-day from within, out of the ego in man, which through Christ experiences its resurrection from the dead.

It is of the greatest importance just here that we should work at ourselves in exactly the right way. With each " I am " we may represent to ourselves that we are wrapped in the greater Ego of Christ. It surrounds us like a cloak of light, full of purity and goodness. And our meditation consists in this, that we are ever saying " yes " to this ego. To say " yes " to Christ, means in the Biblical sense " to believe." And our meditation is an active acquiring of this " belief." We do not need to think of details about Christ—we may also do that, so long as by it we do not get away from that which is central. But we may also bring to activity a continuous assent in our soul for this Ego of Christ, as we first find it. Perhaps we shall be able at first to think only of the " historical Jesus," or of divinity in general. Then let us remain there in that until something more arises for us.

But by experience we know that it is not at all good simply to assent to this higher ego. That easily becomes numb and wearisome. But one may take pains to assent ever more strongly, in an ever more living and exclusive way to experience this ego with one's whole person, and to let oneself be more and more penetrated by it. One will thus gradually learn that there are degrees of this penetration of which one had not even a distant idea. So awake, so sure, so enduring, so spiritual, so living can the presence of a higher ego be in the soul, as if really a spirit were filling its temple. The power of meditation, or we might also say the power of reverence, awakes in us undreamed of things, when we practise them. This fact alone throws a remarkable light upon the talk of those who say that from pure reverence to God we ought not to "practise" in the religious sphere. At the very least this is the talk of inexperience. But in such talk there lies an unconscious crime against humanity.

If we exert ourselves, we need have no anxiety if at first we do not seem to succeed in holding fast throughout our daily life the mood of meditation. Rudolf Steiner, who had most experience in this sphere, even advised that one should not try to hold fast the mood of meditation throughout our daily life. This has especial reference to the occult exercises of the Anthroposophical way of perception. The clear, calm view of everyday events must on no account be lost, if a man would undertake his "higher development." Otherwise he would become an unskilled dreamer. For the religious exercises also, which we here advise, it would be an error to imagine that one can hold fast throughout the whole day the high mood of the quarter-of-an-hour's meditation, that one should feel unhappy if one does not succeed, and that one should long for the quiet quarter-of-an-hour. It is much more important to meditate as strongly as possible, but then, after one has recapitulated it once more, and driven home the result of the meditation, to let it drop and give oneself up whole-heartedly to daily life—with the "I" which now lives in us. One thus delivers the meditation up to death—but also experiences its resurrection.

This does not mean that we could not often in the course of the day recall the highest that was alive in us. On the contrary, one might propose, at least every time the clock strikes the hour, consciously to recall to life the highest that was contained in our meditation. But this purpose is difficult to carry out. It is still better to return into the temple before every new piece of work which we begin, and to pass out to this work from thence. But even this can scarcely be done. We are not yet so strong and so well-trained inwardly that we are able to do that which will be a matter of course to men of later times. Our inner life is weak in comparison with the outer life which constantly oppresses us. We shall learn only gradually to live consciously out of the higher ego, which is formed in meditation.

It ought not even to vex us if we are disturbed in meditation itself, perhaps at its best moment. It is a proof of our inner training if we are always able to come calmly and peacefully out of our meditation when a summons from the outer world reaches us. If we cannot do this, then something in our meditation is not in order. Soon there develops in us ourselves the feeling that we are spoiling again the best that has come or shall come to us, if at this moment we do not remain quiet and joyful. Even when we stand before the door which leads to a higher experience, the calm of spirit which we have acquired by meditation, and which we ought to bring out of our meditation into daily life, should be more important and stronger for us than any particular thing which we were about to acquire. If we succeed in this, then our fellow men will receive only good through our meditation.

Here now we may answer the question : Can one meditate *too much* ? Certainly one can. If so much time is devoted to meditation that one neglects one's duty for it, or if one thereby becomes a stranger to ordinary life, or falls into a dozing state, then there is no longer any profit in meditation, but it may become harmful to ourselves and others. No one can be excused from guarding himself against these dangers. We can give no more than general hints here. One can only say : See whether you become more capable ; see whether your mind becomes clearer and stronger. Life itself will tell you clearly enough whether you are upon the right way. In the physical life one cannot tell anyone how much he may eat, or how much he ought to eat; one can only advise him to develop such a keen perception of his bodily condition, that this itself will tell him, and it will tell him clearly enough. So it is in the life of the soul.

Having made this restriction, we shall continue to say much more about meditation. And we are of the opinion that as long as thousands of people have still so much time to solve crossword puzzles ; *i.e.* to meditate upon them, so long will there be hundreds to meditate upon an " I am." And as long as there are hundreds of thousands willing to hear that " all is quiet on the western front," so long will there be thousands willing to hear that new truth is coming from the Gospel.

When we meditate upon the saying about the resurrection, we are in the happy case of finding that the gospel itself offers us a complete meditation in the story of the raising of Lazarus. We ourselves are resting in the grave of the earth. We may feel our skeleton to be the vault in which we are entombed. *We* are he who is sick; but we are also he " whom the Lord loves," and Martha and Mary also are in our own soul. Doubt and sorrow—truly out of these two forces in the soul the two earthly philosophies of death, scepticism and pessimism, have arisen. Even the more conventional lament which adapts itself to the sorrowful circumstances without rightly feeling their meaning, is present in the story. It is represented by the weeping Jews. One may become conscious of this saying of Christ: " I am the resurrection," in the morning as one awakes. And there may come to be people who will make it a law of their lives to awake at this saying of Christ, as Lazarus awoke in the grave at Bethany—Christ passes us, calls to us and awakes us. If we experience this, the result is an indescribable sanctification of our awakening. The word which was first spoken to Martha : " I am the resurrection and the life," built itself like a new world around Lazarus, who lay there in the grave before the redeeming call came. So can the ego of Christ enwrap us in meditation before the awakening word itself is spoken.

We then experience fully and really that out of this " I " resurrection and life flow. We feel most decidedly that out of this " I " a new world is born, which is different, quite different, from the world of death in which we live. This world is much brighter, more living, more spiritual, more irradiated by this " I." It is not presumption, it is the real acceptance of this saying of Christ, of this deed of Christ, when we try to experience for ourselves this miracle of Lazarus in the very elementary way in which it is possible to experience it at first. Christ does not actually say only at Lazarus' grave : "I am the resurrection and the life," but He always says so, this is always said out of His personality when we have His living presence with us. It is *He*, not one of His sayings.

If we feel this, then we also know where our future lies. *He* is the future of humanity and the future of the world. Now for the first time we recognise clearly that men think quite wrongly of the future. They *hope* for the future or they *fear* the future. We ought to create the future. In all our thinking about the future the story of Lazarus can help us. Everywhere we see the grave, and the sickness unto death, in the world of nations as well as the physical world, in the fate of individuals as well as in a general survey of our times. Everywhere, in front of the grave, stands Christ. And we need only enter into His " I " with our hearing and our feeling, and then the new world comes forth from Him. This world does not come of

itself, it comes out of the " I am " of Christ. But this
"I am" desires to break into our "I am," to break through
it, and it can break into the old world only through our
" I." Thus our relationship to the future will become
different—will become active and heroic.

Now we see how we must work, so that we may gain
the right view of the future, in details, and also as a
whole. It does not come of itself. And our strongest
inward impressions are not strong enough to do everything. We must bring our will into activity, for we can
resolve to do so. But then we are only at the beginning.
A woman once said to me : " If Christianity demands of
me love of my enemy, then I give up Christianity on the
spot." But one gets an ever finer feeling for the fact
that, as a Christian, one must never and in no way think
of the future " as the heathen do," that Christianity must
be in our glance when we look at the world. Not that
we should quote texts from the Bible on every occasion ;
not that we should " simply commit the future to God"
(that is Mohammedanism, but not Christianity), but that
in us is present the *will of Christ who stood at the grave of
Lazarus*. And the earth itself is everywhere *the* grave.
It is a very sacred feeling when in us a piece of the world
is redeemed, because the light of Christ shines into the
darkness of our future. One feels immediately how much
the " penetration by Christ " is advanced. Let one but
notice constantly how a mighty new world springs up—
there is no better way of putting it—out of the " I " of
Christ, out of the inner centre of His life, and one will
experience concretely what the " New Jerusalem " is, and
how the "New Jerusalem " comes into being. As in the
atom there is the whole system of suns, so in our " I "
the " New Jerusalem " is there.

Then two kinds of Christianity are no longer possible :
a Christianity which looks for a world catastrophe,

whereas in the inward parts, in the "I," the great catastrophe, the great revolution is going on, and a Christianity which waits for a beyond, whereas this beyond is breaking into the here and now. But just as impossible for us, when we look again to the East and to the West, is a view of the world such as we find in the East, which desires to redeem men out of this world of death, whereas Christ is the resurrection within the "I," and a view of the world such as we find in the West, which looks for the end of life in the destruction of the world by fire, whereas Christ is life proceeding out of the "I." We shall sometimes, as we practise our meditation, have the feeling as if within us there were pure joy of the resurrection. Everything is full of resurrection music, as if in us the angels themselves were singing over the open grave. Then we begin to have an idea of what Easter is and of how little men have allowed the resurrection Christianity, of which John's Gospel speaks, to become a reality. Perhaps what we have said may also help people to whom this world is still strange to feel and to find reality in their own way.

As we now pass over to the next saying of Christ: "I am the way, the truth, and the life" (John xiv, 6), we are again standing before one of the mighty words of Christ, which alone might be matter for the meditation of a lifetime. The context in which this saying is spoken is especially interesting. Thomas says to Christ: "We know not whither Thou goest, and how can we know the way?" Now it is remarkable how this Thomas, of whom the later legends record that he became the apostle of India, is, in the whole manner of his being, related to the spirit of India. He feels strongly the destiny of death (John xi, 16). He is the melancholy brooder and doubter who longs for sight (John xx, 25). And here at the place we are considering he asks for the "way," as the Indians for thousands of years have asked for the " path," as Sundar Singh and Ghandi to-day, each in their own manner, ask for the way. The saying of Christ in reply to the question of Thomas contains a most remarkable indication of the " mission " to India, which is not yet fully understood. Buddha showed a path, but the saying : " We know not whither Thou goest " is true of him also. When he was asked what Nirvana is, he was silent. " Concerning that, the lofty one revealed nothing " say the Indian texts.

The Indians were the people who did not wish to enter the earthly world, the world of the senses. Dr. Rudolf Steiner has given an illuminating demonstration of this. The Indian is afraid before outward reality. This is expressed in the word itself upon which they meditate, " a-u-m." In the sound " a " the sight is opened to reality. In " u " one is afraid before it. And in " m " one passes over into meditation, into inward humming and musing. In truth the Indian seeks his way back into Paradise. He seeks to perceive that which lies beneath all things, that which comes before them. And he seeks to unite himself with this all-inclusive being, which is there before the multiplicity of appearances. And so he seeks in his own way the tree of knowledge, and the tree of life. And now Christ says, if we put His saying in this way, as it might be spoken to such men : You seek the way back into Paradise ? You seek the tree of knowledge, the tree of life ? You cannot go back. But Paradise has opened and is seeking its lost children upon earth. I am the way ! In my " I " you will find Paradise again ! I am the truth ! In my " I " you will regain the fruits of the tree of knowledge ! I am the life ! In my " I " shall you also have the fruits of the tree of life ! The two trees are no longer separated, but united in my " I."

When we look at this saying from this historical point of view, we can easily derive from it that which sanctifies the past also, our own past, as well as the past of humanity. We here mean by the past, not that which passes away but that which stands. " Eternally still stands the past." We mean that which is the divine background of existence for our being and our life. If we can rise to the contemplation of this, then the past is redeemed from the transitoriness under which men have always suffered so bitterly.

When we look back with such a glance upon our past, we clearly recognise that it divides itself into two parts. The one part is transitory and can by no means be recalled. That is the past which always brings to us the " sorrow for the past." But from the friction of our experiences, the truths we have gained emerge : the victories we have gained in life. That is the eternal part of our past. We must bring this out of the dark mine of the past up into the daylight, and make it fruitful. Christ can help us to do this. He gives us the right way of looking at it. He is " the way " to the Father. For in these truths, these victories we have won from life, the divine being of the Father is looking at us.

And so this saying of Christ may be to us a word for the evening, as the saying about the resurrection is a word for the morning. The most fruitful review of our day is that which can be made under the guidance of this saying. Naturally the saying has many other meanings, and permits of many other different expositions of itself. But what we urgently require is inward work upon our past, daily if possible. It lies there like a great mound of rubbish from which we must recover grains of gold. If we have Christ in us, if we have the will to acquire the greater " I " which lives in peace and works in love, then our past begins to transmute itself into gold. We see the governance of the Father, and begin again to find our way back into the Paradise where we " walk with God."

We therefore resolve that, led by the higher " I " of Christ, we shall go back at evening through our past day, and seek the truths that have revealed themselves to us during the past day, seek to bring home that harvest for our life which has been given to us during the past day. " And the Lord walked in the garden in the cool of the day." (Gen. iii, 8.) We can hold this meditation under the figure that we are walking in Paradise and are eating of the tree of knowledge and of the tree of life. This is sufficient to make the meditation take a quite personal form. We shall see how marvellously such an evening walk with Christ through the past day ennobles our life, even when we learn nothing at all that is individual or new. We receive ever new ideas of what a man may and ought to draw from his life, and what his backward look after death will be. All that is difficult and dark in our life will be redeemed, and will let its secret gold shine forth when it is raised into the bright realm of " truth " and " life." It would be a great step forward if in this way we also learned to walk in the garden of humanity's historical past—I am the way—and there to see the divine truth—I am the truth—and to find the divine life—I am the life. This will be the last history book of humanity : that humanity will be shown how their history has been a way *to* Christ, and therefore, in a higher sense, also a way *with* Christ, in which He was ready to reveal Himself as the truth, and to give Himself as the life. The gospel and all that which Christ reveals in it as truth and life, are as a lamp to this path through the history of humanity.

The earth is the place, so anthroposophical spiritual science says, in which the ego develops towards freedom, so that it may end in love. " I am the way," says Christ concerning this " development." " And the truth," out of that grows " freedom." " And the life," therein lies " love."

Again two kinds of Christianity are no longer possible. A Christianity is impossible which looks upon the personal past only as on that which must be forgiven ; when all the time truth and life are waiting to be won from it. And a Christianity is impossible which looks only at the " story of salvation " in Palestine as a thing of the past ; whereas Christ is the way which must *now* be gone towards truth and light. And in the same way we pass beyond a point of view which prevailed in the East, in which that which is passing in the world was too exclusively seen, and not that which is becoming and remaining ; and we also pass beyond a view to which the West is inclined, in which the past is studied and honoured as if it itself remained and were valuable to humanity, and as if it were not a way to truth and life.

And now there still remains the present for us to discuss. Often men say : " Holy is the present." This is said in all possible keys. But a practicable way to the inward consecrating of the present is seldom shown. In this sense, we can find no more fruitful saying than the last " I am " of John's Gospel : " I am the true vine and My Father is the husbandman, and ye are the branches." (John xv, 1 and 5.)

This saying presupposes a quite different way of regarding the world from that which we usually have. The history of mankind does not proceed in such a way that from beginning to end there is a continuous development. That is the heathenish error which is fundamental to our age's consciousness of the world. But the earth was the field prepared beforehand ; " my Father is the field labourer " says the Greek text of this sublime parable of the history of the world. But one day a seed of light struck down into the field from above, and since then the duty of the earth has been to help this seed of light to unfold itself. And when it is unfolded, then the old dark earth may fall away. Its task is accomplished. In this image we see world history *in truth*. Christ is the seed of light who wills to become the tree of life upon this field of the world.

Thus we understand the saying : " Apart from me ye can do nothing " (John xv, 5). We become conscious that all we do when out of Christ and without Him, is in the deepest sense " nothing." It does not come into consideration in respect of the true development of humanity. We become conscious that the real fruits for the development of humanity are only where his life-blood flows : " Herein is My Father glorified that ye bear much fruit : so shall ye be My disciples " (John xv, 8). We become aware that every branch must be purified if it is to bring forth more fruit—the meaning of our sorrows becomes apparent—and that all the branches that do not bring forth fruit must, somehow and sometime, be cast out of the true development of the world (John xv, 2). We also become aware that the real life stream in the vine—the life stream from Christ—is *joy* (John xv, 11). In this joy is strength to bring forth the right fruits. Nietzsche is right in saying that men have rejoiced too little, if one takes this saying of his Zarathustra in such a connection. It is truth : out of the depths of union with Christ there first flows true strength and joy into every moment of the present. And on the other hand, where this strength and joy is, come valuable fruits as if of themselves. The branch need do no more than become permeable by the sap of the vine. This sap will of itself ripen to fruit by the sun of life. A branch is the most unpretending thing there is, but it is at the same time a precious work-shop, in which the sap of the vine changes into fruit. The fruit may be much greater and better than the branch, if this fruit is created entirely by the vine ; that concerns the vine and the fruit. If one once lives earnestly in this Christlike feeling for life, then one will see how sound it is, how refreshing and how productive of life. That which has come forth out of the vine as fruit will one day become the real fruits of earth's development.

When a man in the course of his daily life remembers often his existence as a branch; when he sees his individual work in this connection with the world—the seed of light in the earth, which must grow to be the tree of life—and brings his life into the ordered scheme of this great connection with the world : when he, wherever he is, seeks to do his work and brings his fruit out of such a union with life ; when he thinks thus in a living way of Christ—that he is there only for the sap of life which flows into him through Christ; when he can let the " I am " of Christ really flow through him as a new life sap—then will he be able to live rightly at *every* moment, and his *present* will become *holy*. One day he will remember the promise of Christ : " I shall no more drink of the fruit of the vine till the day when I drink it new in my Father's kingdom." And it will seem to him as if he had already entered into the fulfilment of this saying. His new method of work will place him in the beginnings of " the Father's kingdom " and his union with Christ will be a " drinking of the fruit of the vine." The ego of Christ is a most subtle and a most noble life sap : the life sap of a new world.

And so man will acquire a new view of the present state of the world around him. He will believe that the fruits of Christ are not only there where His name is named, but also there where His life sap flows. And he will acquire the true perception of this sap of life. Therefore he will recognise much to be in connection with Christ, which is not known to be such by men. But on the other hand he will have the terrible power of recognising where fruits are growing which must inevitably go to destruction.

We propose that a man should not only sometimes have such thoughts, but that he should explicitly practise this meditation at least now and then—that he feels himself as a humble branch of the new vine which the husbandman plants, that he drinks from the vine and thinks of the fruits into which he leads all which he can receive only from the vine, for whose sake he exists.

A false Christianity condemns the present and lives either in the past or in the future. From both we are free, from the Eastern way of living to which the present is nothing, and from the Western way to which it is all.

The future—a resurrection from the grave, the past— a walking in the garden of paradise, the present—a drinking of the fruit of the vine. Under such pictures we hallow time as we have before hallowed space. The darkly flowing river of time becomes a holy stream when we let this sun shine upon it. We can in a spiritual sense do that which the Indian does in outward cult, when he bathes in the holy river Ganges, and purifies himself. We shall have the experience that thus we *redeem time*.

But it will be good if one does not only go through the individual meditations according to one's need, and their character, but if at times one chooses a day, say an early Sunday morning, when one goes through them *all*. When one has previously been through the individual meditations, one need not remain so long over each single one. Then one will discover how entirely new a world is around one. We shall recognise that we are upon the way to a " Christian outlook upon the world," in a much higher sense than we have understood the phrase before. We shall see that we are everywhere upon the track of high perception, on the path to the development of the life of perception in the sense of John's Gospel. "This is life eternal to know Thee, the only true God, and Jesus Christ whom Thou has sent," and on the path to a hallowing of the spiritual being in the sense of the first petition of the Lord's Prayer: "Hallowed be Thy Name!" We shall bear this petition about in us differently, illuminated by the content of Christ's announcement: "I have manifested Thy Name unto them."

And at the same time we shall find that we ourselves now receive our real "I." When we pass through the revelation of the "I" of Christ, we see for the first time the full meaning of a holy "I." The present age is sick, simply with the sickness of the ego. We cannot go back to the time before the ego, and we cannot content ourselves with railing against the egoism of our race. We can only go forward to the true ego. The men of the present age must be brought to that which "healeth the self in the depths of the soul," as it says in the Easter prayer of the Act of Consecration of Man. Each "I am" contains a healing herb for one sickness of the ego: "I am the bread" gives help against self-love of the ego; "the light" against fear of the ego; "the good shepherd" against weakness of the ego; "the door" against cramping of the ego; "the resurrection" heals numbness of the ego; "the way, the truth and the life" heals impoverishment of the ego; "the true vine" heals self-seeking, self-willed hardening of the ego. But beyond all these single sicknesses of the ego, concerning which a whole book might be written, when we are living positively in these seven sayings we receive our higher ego, which is entirely a part of Christ and is yet our own self as we ought to be. Just there is the miracle.

One may also, when in the early hours of Sunday one goes through the seven " I ams," be justified in representing to oneself that one is receiving all the seven sacraments spiritually. "I am the way, the truth and the life," that is Baptism. " I am the true vine, ye are the branches," that is Confirmation ; " I am the good shepherd," that is Confession ; "I am the door," that is Marriage ; " I am the bread," that is the Last Supper, " I am the light of the world," that is Consecration of Priests ; " I am the resurrection and the life," that is the Last Sacrament. When we think that the first " I am " speaks of *bread*, and the last of *wine*, we feel that there is a communion in these " I ams," a way of dedication, a sacred service of God, which must be found out, of which only a very little can be said.

" I in the Father and the Father in Me," that is the central proclamation of John's Gospel. It is continued in us when Christ in His high-priestly prayer says, " I in them ! " (John xvii, 21-26.) "I in the Father," to that we are inwardly trained by the four first " I ams," through which we learn to live in the ego of the Father as in a new space. " The Father in Me—in the ego," *that* is formed in us by the three last " I ams," when with this new " I " we enter into the new time. One dives deep into the ground of the world when on all sides, in all four spiritual directions, one meets the face of the Father's " ego," which is everywhere, " love." " No man hath seen God at any time ; the only begotten Son, which is in the bosom of the Father, He hath declared Him." (John i, 18.) And one " unites with the world's evolving " as it says in the Act of Consecration of Man, when one lets the three last " I ams " grow into reality, and so receives that which can be truly called " peace."

87

And so the seven sayings are united to our basic meditation of peace and love.

When we spoke above of the Indians, we saw that their whole attitude to the world is expressed in the word on which they meditate " a-u-m." A totally different attitude to the world lies in the Hebrew " ani," which is the Hebrew word for " I." Here also is reality felt, " a," but then it passes—we see the other direction clearly—into the " n," which contains the negation of the reality just given, the opposite negation to that of the Indians. It is no retreat, it is a breaking through. In " i," the sound which expresses the light of the inwardness of the ego, appears the new reality. The Hebrew says as it were to the reality which surrounds him (and that was his difference from the " heathen " around him) : " Thou art not that which I seek ; I must tear myself away from thee : I must negate thee." In the ego comes a new reality from within. In the Hebrew race especially the " ego " in humanity had to be formed. Still more laboriously, more darkly and more stubbornly does the ego work itself through in the other Hebrew word for " I " : " anoki."

But as it were a new world shines forth in the German word : " Ich." The " i " sound begins the word. But this " i " turns back to the world and gives itself to it. In the " ch " it spreads itself sacrificially over the world. And so in the German word " Ich " we can find our basic meditation expressed in its two sounds, and can unite this word in its sound with our basic meditation, in a living way. In the " i " is the purity of divine peace. In the " ch " the self-sacrifice of divine love.

It would be a favourable sign of the reality of our meditation if we learned to say this word " I " with different feelings in everyday life. The evangelist John would not use the word " I " for himself, after he had heard it in the mouth of Christ. He calls himself only by a circumlocution " the disciple whom Jesus loved." We live in the time of self-seeking, and of false dark perception. We must redeem this time, and redeem it first in ourselves. Then we learn to speak the word " I " in a new way, with our speech indeed, but above all, with our whole being ; to speak it in such a way that Christ is in it with His peace and love.

VI

" IN the evening at all events you must take a portion of
Holy Scripture with you in your thoughts to bed,
which you may ruminate like a clean animal, and go softly
to sleep. But it ought not to be much, but rather quite a
small portion, thoroughly well-pondered and understood ;
and when you rise in the morning you shall find it as a
bequest from yesterday."

How many readers will recognise that we have here
before us a saying of Luther about meditation ? He
writes it to the pastor in his "*ratio vivendi sacrorum*"
(how priests ought to live). In this saying, as often in
Luther's writings, two periods of time meet. From his
Catholic past he had still a connection with meditation,
which was practised very earnestly in the monasteries.
But in this saying a comfortable bourgeois Christianity
also reveals itself, which afterwards became the danger of
Protestantism. Not much can be felt in it of the heroic
effort, which distinguishes every real meditation. Luther
indeed knew this heroic effort especially in prayer. But
still, it is quite obvious that something else pushes its
way in.

And yet the figure of rumination is noteworthy,
although the sphere from which it is taken is lowly. In
meditation a saying or a picture is actually permeated with
the substance of our own human being, and permeates us
with the substance of its own being. The more strongly
we are able to meditate the more does the latter permea-
tion occur. A spiritual process of taking in takes place.

It is the same process as in Luther's picture, only upon a

higher plane. Therefore many a figure like this can reveal exactly the right way to meditate. And when one adds " thoroughly well-pondered and understood," that also is something which belongs to true meditation. Luther's summons was not, certainly, the impulse to a new age of meditation. But many a one who has loved, and who still loves, evangelical Christianity in its best form may be helped by the indication that we in this place see a new religious age growing out of Luther, which Luther himself could not bring in, but to which there was an approach in him. With the phrase "ruminating like a clean animal," Luther calls already to the far-off Darwin. Instead of it one must say " penetrated with being, like an angel " and one would then call up a new age.

Here let us go into the question which a young reader of these letters who has power in meditation asks, namely, whether meditation immediately on awakening from sleep is not dangerous, because man in a horizontal position is quite different from man in an upright position. Being more in a state of metabolism, of change and repair in his system, in this position he may indeed easily have spiritual experiences, but they come in a dreamlike way out of his lower life system. This danger is certainly there, and it is good to be aware of it. In ancient India this would have been still more clearly felt. But the result of European development is such that man becomes to a high degree independent of outward things, and also of his bodily position. The question is simply *if one is able* to meditate strongly in a spiritual way when lying down. And it is a fact of experience that it is possible to do so, though in most cases not without practice and effort. One will notice oneself that it is a help if one at least lays one's head higher, without bringing oneself out of the spiritual mood of the night. Especially, in so far as one wants to bring the deeper experiences of the night into one's consciousness, it will be well not to change the bodily position too much. Let each seek to find out what is possible for him. In any case, the right thing is that the meditation should take place, not in a consciousness below the level of the daily consciousness, but in a stronger, more awakened, clearer consciousness than the everyday consciousness, or that it should lead into such a consciousness. And to what degree the human consciousness can become clear and spiritual, one has at first no idea.

This is above all true for the meditations to which we are now coming. If the seven " I ams " were above all a sanctifying of thought, we now turn especially to the sanctifying of feeling. What is taking place to-day to ennoble human feeling ? Much is done unconsciously by art. And it would be possible, from the great works of art to build up a system of self-training similar to that which we have just built up out of John's Gospel. He who would daily allow the Sistine Madonna of Raphael, in colour if possible, to work upon him for five minutes, would be completely changed in three years. The pure divine-humanity of this picture—one can call it nothing else—would pour its essence into him.

If pictures have a very strong action upon the life of feeling, yet the strongest pictures, those that act most powerfully, are the occurrences which the gospels afford us in the form of the acts of Christ. No master in the world has ever painted them worthily. We shall have clearly recognised this at the end of our studies. But it is perhaps good that we must ourselves inwardly picture these scenes. They thus become freer, more stirring, more personal and still richer in mystery than if a master had first passed them through his soul for us.

By nothing can our life of feeling be more cleansed,

changed, made divine, than when we go the old well-trod way through the seven last stations of Christ's perfecting. But we go this way quite differently from the mediæval monks. In the cloisters, before one plunged into the sorrows and resurrection of Christ, one had first for twelve weeks to allow the twelve preceding chapters of John's Gospel to act upon one. In them, the first five " I ams " were contained. But it is something different when one has first conquered the " I " for oneself, as we have sought to do. One remains then more protected against what is merely feeling, and enters much more into what is spiritual. Simply because free thinking was still dulled, Christian feeling in the Middle Ages was developed to a height which was marvellously great and pure. That was exactly the task of this period of history. If we wish not to lose this, but to win it anew, it can only proceed to-day from the awake, conscious, strong " I," which the new age has made possible. In this way the whole life of feeling receives another character, a greater spirituality and an inclusiveness of the world.

If we look at our life of feeling, we soon see clearly that it is very much in need of cleansing and of self-training. And out of the feeling proceeds the will. Although the life of feeling seems to be very much our own individual possession, entirely shut up in ourselves, yet it is just as much the mother earth from which our whole life grows up. A soul which is filled with noble feeling, if these feelings are healthy and strong, does not need to trouble about leading a good life.

Now a man might train his inner life by taking one feeling after another and to some extent visualising it. But it is much more profitable and surer to guide powerful new feelings into the soul, and let them wash away or wash through what is already there. Even to him, to whom Christ is not yet what he is to us, the passion of

Christ will bring that reverence which makes it possible to go with Christ in some wise.

The new feeling which has come into the world through Christianity is called *Love*. Let one only read writings of pre-Christian times and notice that his sun had simply not yet risen. Even in Buddhism, in its benevolent kindness to all creatures, there is only the first red of the morning.

But love has entered into the souls of men in such a way that it has intermingled with everything which was already there. And so it has itself become clouded, so that it is scarcely recognisable. That is true of very much which is called " Christian Love." Often enough to-day one has the impression that it is not Christian love which has changed hearts, but that hearts have changed Christian love. Often it is a false zeal for proselytizing which takes no heed of another's freedom, and so neither sees nor reaches his real ego ; often a sentimental feeling which only spoils the word " love " for men. Sometimes it is a new kind of occupation, in which a man is really escaping from himself, sometimes, also, an evil curiosity which pushes itself into everything. Not seldom it is a slavish losing of one's self, which one then calls " selfless devotion," not seldom also an assertion of one's self, in which, under the name of Christlikeness, one wishes to have all men the same as oneself. It is sad to observe how, under the mask of Christian love, the most hateful egotism spreads itself abroad, and never thinks of putting itself into other men's place, much less of dying into them. Nothing to-day more requires thorough cleansing than Christian love itself.

The high, pure spirit of the love of Christ has as yet been scarcely seen or felt. And yet, just in respect of love, Christ has most deliberately and most clearly given definite teaching, as if he had foreseen all the

94

dangers of which we are speaking. We need only think of how seldom He takes the word love into His mouth, and in what connection He then uses it. How, when love is the subject of the talk, He at once tells the parable of the Good Samaritan, the parable in which is contained a whole catechism of love, but tells it not in the form of teaching, but as a picture, as an action. Or how He Himself, at the end of His life, before He speaks of love itself as of a new commandment for His disciples, gives as practical instruction to His disciples themselves the *Washing of the Feet*.

All this may help us to draw near with right attention to the first station of Christ's way. Here again, as we have done up till now, we shall not enter too much into the details of the building up of the meditation, but will only give hints. Thus the individual is left free to build up meditation as he chooses. And he will have his own experiences and find his personal way. If, as some would like, we carried out the suggestions into their exact details, the reader would have difficulty in getting away from the details, would experience a kind of stereotyping of the pictures, and would not so easily make them entirely his own, so that they can develop further in a living way. The reader cannot be spared the trouble of doing this. But this advice may be given : that one should first place the story of the Washing of the Feet (John xiii, 1-35) before one's soul in a living way and take it into oneself. It is given to us for this purpose. With all its details, the narrator has stamped it upon his own soul : Jesus rose, laid aside His upper garment, took a towel and girded Himself. So was the Master dressed like a slave. All these details have gradually become significant and transparent for the evangelist.

But all the details ought only to lead on to the great chief event, to the wonderful spirit of service, which there reveals itself in Christ. If one has penetrated to a lively feeling of this spirit, one may represent to oneself that one is breathing this spirit in, as one drinks in the air when one breathes deeply. According to the investigations of spiritual science, feeling is most nearly connected with the so-called " middle man," with the man who lives above all in the " rhythmic " system of the lungs and heart. One can indeed with this very meditation on feeling go actually through all the five senses, raising them all to a higher plane. In the Jesuit exercise, the *exercitia spiritualia* of Ignatius Loyola, hell is experienced in all the senses successively, as one first sees in imagination the torment of the damned, then hears their crying, then smells the smoke, and so on. But here, in such meditations as the foot-washing one can really perceive heaven as with higher senses. And one is not obliged to think that one must have first passed separately through hell if one is to become fully capable of receiving heaven, but with heaven one experiences a hell at the same time, as far as one carries it within oneself, the being in which evil rages, the being which is certainly not heaven.

When one has first made the picture of the Washing of the Feet clear for the spiritual eye, then one may seek to receive the being of Christ with the spiritual ear as a marvellous sound, then to breath in the smell of the sacrifice, then—as in the biblical saying : " Taste and see how gracious the Lord is "—to experience the taste of such an action as if with the tongue, and lastly, to touch the act quite concretely and spiritually and pass into the warm feeling of its life. All this requires practice. But then it gives to man a living impression of a higher world, in which his senses also change. We say this here as being applicable to all meditations on pictures, and now turn again to the picture before which we are standing.

As a motto beneath the Washing of the Feet stands the saying in the Bible : " The princes of this world exercise dominion—but the Son of Man is come not to be ministered unto but to minister and to give His life a ransom for many," only that in the place of " Son of Man " in Matthew's Gospel, in the sense of John's Gospel the word " I " might be placed," *I* am come not to be ministered unto but to minister."

In such a word as this, Christ places Himself over against Cæsar, who, at the same point of time in the world's history, appeared in the world to rule it. If we think of this coincidence in time, we begin to see that the ego, as it has to develop in the world, sees before itself two ways—either the way through warfare to power, or the way through freedom to love. Christ and Cæsar are opposed to one another until the end of the days and fight for the ego of man. This historic warfare is waged on our behalf also. The saying of Christ just quoted contains a final historic decision and a challenge to Cæsar which could not be more evident. In this decisive opposition we have in a sublime way the same thing which, perhaps out of the mysteries, was represented to men as the opposition between heavenly and earthly love. And one can find this struggle nowhere more impressively than in the history of Rome itself ! Christ has driven Cæsar from his throne in Rome, but in spite of this, Cæsar has again and again fallen upon Christ in Rome and driven Him away. The papacy is a battle between Cæsar and Christ. Cæsar, the household tyrant, the terror to subordinates, the self-asserter and self-avenger, must be rooted out of every corner of our lives. After ascending the throne, princes issue a proclamation to their peoples. Also, after Christ has ascended the throne a royal message follows to all who are willing to belong to Him, " a new commandment give I to you, that ye

97

love one another, as I have loved you. By this shall all men know that ye are my disciples, if ye have love one to another." If one actively places oneself before this decision, one has the same decision to make with the world as the Jesuits have in their placing King Lucifer in Babylon over against King Christ in Jerusalem. In its connection with the Gospels this decision is more inward and has greater content.

We do not wish to give here an exposition of the Bible, but only to create a mood as background for the meditation upon the Washing of the Feet. One ought to feel very strongly the kingliness of this love. Then love will lose the smallness, the pettiness and the slavishness which it still has in the Christian world. Christ was anxious that this kingliness should be felt, " Ye call me master and lord, and ye say well, for so I am. If I then, your Lord and Master, have washed your feet ; ye ought also to wash one another's feet." Only he who feels this kingliness, this divineness *of Love itself*, will become quite free from that secret desire for recognition and gratitude. He knows that such love is the only possible divine attitude towards all beings. For the highest God has nothing above him, but everything under him. His life can only consist in this that he turns to those who are under him. One has not yet any real divine life within one if one does not feel that God seeks in us also those who need help. Only in the kingdom of love does one find that God is really in us.

If through this a new kind of pride could be aroused in man as he is, a pride which would be by reason of this the more horrible, Christ does away with this pride, by setting about the most humble action with this royal love, yes, by first doing this most humble act before he speaks. He does not first say : " Ye ought to love one another " but " Ye ought to wash one another's feet." As if to

98

guard for ever against all pride, He sets His example before the disciples : " That ye do as I have done to you." In just such fine traits one feels the spirit of Christ.

" As I have done to you "—the words sound so full of meaning. Can one perhaps grasp the meaning of the whole of Christ's deed for humanity under the figure of the Washing of the Feet ? This can best be done by calling in the help of certain concepts of spiritual science. Man, through his fall, has sunk down to earth, having before been much less developed but much more spiritual. The earth, upon which he now wanders, is the place of sin. From beneath, from the earth, which has become the sphere of his life, man as a spiritual being soils himself ever more and more—even if evil did not assail him, even if it were not present in himself. And in this way also it comes about that the state of a man's will expresses itself especially in his feet, as well as in his hands. If a man is angry, he clenches his fists and stamps his feet. In a man's walk, the state of his will is more clearly visible than he commonly observes. For example, there is the short, masterful step, and the weak, shambling shuffle. It is not without significance that one speaks of an " impure walk." But Christ came to earth to help men from the very bottom upward. He heals the ground on which man goes. He heals also the feet with which he goes. Follow me ! I am the Way !

As if for a sign that here are deep secrets, two quite different kinds of feet are placed in opposition to one another in the story of the Washing of the Feet. " He that eateth bread with me hath lifted up his heel against me." One need only take this word in the most obvious sense of the words in the Hebrew original : " He who is my guest lifts his heel against me." It is also a picture of Cæsar. He sits at the divine table, a guest, like all the others, but in his self-exaltation he at

99

the same time spurns the earth upon which he lives, and thus insults the spirit of the earth.

From this we understand the remarkable fact, which Rudolf Steiner mentions in his lectures on John's Gospel, that the mystics of the Middle Ages, when they entered fully into the experience of the Washing of the Feet, really believed that they felt water poured around their feet. The modern psychologist will here have no hesitation in talking about suggestion. It may have occurred here and there. In reality, another process, which is entirely holy, is often at the bottom of this. When a man unites himself entirely to Christ, he loses this egotistical spurning of the mother earth upon which he stands. He plunges, particularly with his feet also, into an active spirituality. For only for a purely external way of thinking are the feet so unspiritual and merely corporeal, as one to-day considers them. In them man is united to strong earth forces which he can feel especially in them.

Since Christ has been present in earthly being, these earth forces can be entirely Christianised, can entirely become agents through which the spirit of Christ can work. The picture of this is given in the vision of Christ in the Revelation of John. Christ Himself appears there with feet like molten brass : the strongest of earth forces with the fire of love glowing through them. These mystics experienced the beginning of this ; and the men of to-day can experience it. Then one has the experience of purification from the " ground up."

Some will at first be able only to listen to such evidence. They may, indeed, guess from it that such Biblical pictures contain nothing that is accidental, even in their details. If one surrenders oneself to them, one has not only religious moral experiences in the heart, but goes towards a new world.

But first of all everyone can hear out of the story itself

the voice of Christ—Love means to wash the feet, to take man in his earthly circumstances, and through this deed to help him upwards from beneath. It is still child-like to imitate Christ's example outwardly, as the kings of Bavaria on Holy Tuesday collected some old men in the royal palace, and poured water over their feet— which had been thoroughly cleansed beforehand. It was better when in the Middle Ages certain communities really celebrated the washing of the feet as a sacrament. It is best of all if we, at moments when we have an opportunity of showing love, let this picture arise before our souls : Washing of the Feet—that is the great act of Christ Himself. That is His divine example. We shall then come to have quite other thoughts than if we were wishing to have love as a pleasing feeling in our hearts. From below upwards, to sanctify men from the ground upwards through the act of service : that is Christian love. Many orders of monks in the past had exercises in humility. But the wonderful word humility has many stains on it to-day. We must win it back as a royal will to serve.

If this will lives in us, then we may always strengthen and inspire it again from the picture of Christ, from the example of the Washing of the Feet. Let us then, after we have brought about a right feeling inwardly from a study of the details, look solely at the principal feature, *Christ* as, in this divine will to serve, he washes men's feet—*men's* feet. Let us drink into ourselves this will, this frame of mind, till we are filled with it—if possible so strongly that we think that now through all eternity nothing else could live in us.

During this exercise and the following exercises of this second group, we may feel our ego, as we have gained it from the first group of exercises, to be at last exactly like the vessel of the Grail, which lets itself be filled from above with the noblest content, with the life-blood of Christ himself. It is not that we should outwardly enter a fellowship of the Grail and play with thoughts of the Grail, but that we should inwardly gain the experience of the Grail. The ego can, like an inverted vessel, shut itself off from above, and overshadow others below; then it becomes a Cæsar. Whether a greater Cæsar or a less, depends upon its gifts. The ego can also open itself towards what is above, and give itself as an offering to what is beneath; then it becomes a disciple of Christ. John the Baptist stood at the door to new things; the ego felt itself lonely and empty and called for content. Then came Christ and said, "I am," and now we take into ourselves the essential content of this "I am." That is the experience of the Grail.

Here one sees clearly indeed that this has nothing to do with "mystical" feeling, as one understands mysticism to-day, but is a fundamental form of training for man—as man requires it to-day.

The first thing which we have had to discuss is the divine fundamental frame of mind itself, which Christ brought to earth. For only with Christ is it worth while to live upon earth. With Christ we willingly return every day to earth, however little it pleases us to do so. In the Act of Christ, the highest will of the divine Father of the worlds, which lies at the root of all earthly happenings, is mirrored before us. It was a divine necessity that the Father of the worlds should at some time bring a world into being in which He could express His divine will and power, as He has done in the earth; His most loving aid, even from the lowest depths.

But he who wishes to live upon the earth, must take upon himself the fate of the earth; and so we come to the second stage of inward union with Christ. The first object upon which our gaze fell was man, and the fundamental feeling towards man was the first to be awakened. For earth is there for man. But the second thing is to gaze upon the world, which surrounds men. Here we enter the history of the earth. The word which must lead us into this world is the word *peace*. As love to men had led and leads us, so peace enfolds us in the world.

But Christian peace is just as perverted as Christian love, and just as much in need of cleansing. The manner in which the words " love " and " peace " are alive for the most part to-day in Christianity, has repelled men like Nietzsche. What on the contrary, real peace is in the sense of Christ, can best be learnt from the picture of the *Scourging*. It is not a mediæval peace of the cloister, which withdraws from the world, but just a standing in the midst of the vexations of the world. It is not a Protestant peace of the soul, which lives only in the forgiveness of one's own sin, but an acceptance of the fate of the world in the strength which comes from above. Looking still further out into human history, we see that the heroic indifference of the Stoic, and the spiritually strong absence of desire in the Buddhist, are far behind the picture of heroic Christianity shown in the Scourging.

Here again we think of the Scourging as a figure which sums up all that ever happened to Christ. It is overwhelming to represent to oneself Christ at the pillar of martyrdom, the holy and divine one against whom rough hands directed the blows which lacerated His flesh. Some will doubt whether their " nerves " are trained to stand a serious meditation upon this picture. And yet we enter for the first time into the actual fate of what is divine in the world, when this picture becomes alive in us. It is never otherwise with the divine. He who is not willing for this, may look after small joys, but not the divine in the world. Conversely, the truly divine in the world is proved to be so by its making men strong and courageous to share this fate. It is good to call up this picture of Christ again and again clearly before one. For, as Goethe has said, one can best help oneself in the face of the many renunciations which life demands by "resigning oneself once and for all;" and it will be found that, after such a meditation upon Christ, one returns back into ordinary life much stronger and more courageous. One knows what lies before one, one's resolve has been strengthened and one is *then* surprised to meet so much good in the world. A new meaning of "redemption through Christ" dawns upon us. At the present day one thinks, if one thinks at all of these words, of the act of death once performed by Christ at Golgotha. But from the individual details also of Christ's life redemption continually goes forth. He who has really carried out the meditation on the scourging of Christ, is "redeemed from all querulous complaining, from all illusions about life, from all false hopes and wishes." One notices for the first time that one has carried those about with one unconsciously. One has a completely different attitude to life; one's attitude now is that, as helper of the divine in the world, one can endure life and master it. Christ has taken our sorrows upon Himself; this old point of view acquires a new meaning. There actually proceeds from the picture of Christ a power by which the sorrows which lie before us, as sorrows, are taken away, and His joys are given us in return. Such a concrete experience of "redemption" through Christ, as we here show it in connection with one point only, is weightier and leads us further, than if one carried the old church teaching in one's head, and "believed" in it, as one speaks of "believing" to-day, in the full sense which has no longer much to do with the Biblical meaning.

But from the Scourging one ought to look out at the

whole life of Christ. He who, after a meditation upon
the Scourging, reads the farewell talk in John's Gospel,
will discover that every word interpolated by the disciples
into this revelation of Christ is like a blow from a whip.
Not merely a pin-prick—a real stroke of a scourge.
Then let him read back in John's Gospel how " the
Jews "—one must not here think of the Jews by race—
receive every word, every act of Christ, and it will dawn
upon us that the life of Christ was a tying to a pillar of
martyrdom, and everything, almost everything, that came
from men was a scourging. One does not notice this
only because Christ, for example in His farewell talk, bears
it all so greatly that He transforms it into good. And so,
after reading Christ's farewell talk (John xiii–xvi), when
one has especially observed the inward attitude of Christ
to the interruptions of His disciples, one may add this
inward attitude of Christ, this unassailable greatness of
holiness, vividly to our picture of the Scourging. And
through this it will begin to dawn upon us gradually,
that there may be a " becoming worthy of sharing the
sufferings of Christ." For there is nothing which can
better help humanity forward and redeem it than that one
should bring against the evil attacks of men this high and
noble bearing of Christ, this purity of one who belongs
to God.

The old mystics spoke of " the patience of God." But
when this Godlike patience occurs only in the cloister,
and there refreshes itself with the " divine life," it has not
reached Christ's heights. It must stand against the
frightful enmity of the world, must be an active " uniting "
of oneself with the world's evolving " which can happen
through Christ," must be a free taking upon oneself of
the fate of the divine in human history. One must feel
that this patience, this peace, is the very last quality to be
gained by the struggle of a strong and fiery man. As

one has found that the Greeks valued " Sophrosyne," quietness of mind, because it was hard for them to attain it, so is Christian peace great, when it is the victory of a strong will *over itself*.

Men have at first spoiled everything which they have taken over from Christ. Thus there was a sentimental sympathy with Christ, an outward imitation of His sufferings, well-meant indeed, but often vain and self-seeking, and even at the best, lacking in ultimate greatness. There was also a slavish putting-up with anything in the name of Christ, and other similar things. The meditation of the Scourging can set us free from all these, if we meditate not only in our feelings, but with our ego awakened to the choice before it. We do not imitate the hair-shirts and self-scourging of the monks of old. But we see Christ, bound of his own free will to the world-tree, smitten by men, opposing to all tortures no outward resistance but only His own divine greatness. Then we think ourselves into His position, take His fate of our own free will upon us, and vow that in this spirit we shall stand fast against whatever may come.

In the lectures on St. John's Gospel mentioned above, Rudolf Steiner describes how, in connection with their devoted contemplation of Christ's scourging, the mediæval mystics really had the feeling that they were receiving blows. We have heard of similar experiences at the present time more in the form of dreams which occurred after contemplation of the scourging. Here, again, is an occurrence which need in no way be suggestion. If a man fills himself with Christ, if he raises himself above his narrow personal life and unfolds himself in love to the world, then his finer invisible man actually breaks through the sheath in which it has lived until now. That which has been called the etheric man—

not yet the actual spirit-man, but already the more delicate organ of the spirit-man—begins to take part in a greater life. The first thing which then meets man is that he feels the opposition which comes from all sides, the opposing powers which will not endure the divine. This is the more severely felt just because the man is then living in the feeling that he wishes only to bring good, and in the unconscious supposition that other men must as a matter of course recognise that which to himself is great and divine. For this reason, men who, filled with a great conviction, wished to help their fellow-men, had first to fight against a heightened sensitiveness, when humanity answered them so entirely differently from what they believed they had a right to expect. The experience which we know as " pin-pricks " becomes our experience from the world. These feelings may set in when a man has conscious experience of enmity, and also when he simply feels himself to be a disciple of Christ in the world. They may then be more unconscious or they may be too conscious. They live in a higher spirituality, which can be distinguished well from everyday consciousness.

Thus with a free and loving walking in the world, a scourging is necessarily united. It is verily a sign that a man is growing out of himself upward into a higher life. For this reason Christ appears in Revelation as clothed in the flowing mantle held in by the golden girdle. This picture reveals itself as the opposite picture to the scourging. Only he who knows the sensitiveness described above, which feels itself so helpless in the world, can, by binding his fate, his will, his ego to Christ, Who for His divine ministry was scourged at the world-tree, find security, strength and rest in the face of experiences which lie before him in some form or another. We hold it to be important that we should learn the " peace " of

Christ from *the* Christ Whom we see standing at the stake of torture. Again one may drink in this peace at the end of the meditation, like a noble life-sap from a higher world, when we have allowed the inner picture to lapse. Thus we are ensured against a Luciferic egotistical peace. Thus we can find beforehand " peace " in the right sense, in the face of the fate which we take upon ourselves when we wish to stand for what is divine in the world; in the face of little experiences of everyday life as well as in the face of a final shattering of our outward being.

In these studies we are seeking from Christ himself a purification of Christian qualities, or rather of fundamental Christian frames of mind. We have seen that Christian love is something different from that which men usually understand it to be; so is Christian peace. Now we turn to Christian holiness.

In the Middle Ages, as Rudolf Steiner describes, men experienced the crowning with thorns in this way, that this will rose within them : " I will stand upright against all the world's derision and mocking! I will stand for the holy thing which is entrusted to me! Even if I remain all alone, I will stand undismayed for what is most sacred to me ! " The true Christian holiness is something more individual and more active than it seems to the Catholics to be when they think of " sinlessness," and something deeper and more inward than the Protestants think when they talk of " doing their duty." Every man has his own higher ego, which must first be brought down to earth. In this higher ego, divine revelations slumber which it already bears within itself, and over it hover divine revelations which it can still receive. With every human ego an especial divine thought enters into the world, an especial divine charge, an especial divine gift. This is the true holiness in the sense of Christ : to keep faith with this higher ego, to let this higher ego enter as a sacrifice into the world's evolving; not to imagine for oneself any special mission, but to find out the charge which is given to us as a divine thought in our ego; not to thrust oneself upon men, but to give oneself to humanity. It is clear that it is not here a question of fulfilling commandments, nor merely of avoiding sins. More inward and more personal, but also more heroic and more aggressive, is this new holiness. It is the holiness which we see in Christ. He has not spoken of it in words, but has given it by deeds. For Him there was only one single commandment: The Son of Man must not do anything of himself, but fulfil the charge which the Father has given him.

Here we plunge into depths in which holiness and wisdom are one and the same. For not outward knowledge, but divine wisdom is in our higher ego. The thought of God which we ought to be is, rightly understood, our ultimate wisdom. That deed in our life into which this thought of God will change itself is our true holiness.

So that we may lose all pride arising from this mission from God, we need only gaze at Christ as He stands there in the crown of thorns. Our glance sees not only the horrible brutality, but reads also the sublime word of God which is there spoken to us.

" Thorns and thistles shall it bear unto thee " (the earthly ground) said the history of the beginning of the world in a prophetic saying. Thorns are the badge of the earth with its sorrow and struggle. But out of the burning thorn-bush, out of this earthly field which is full of struggle and sorrow, Jehovah reveals Himself to men. And in the crowning with thorns, Christ takes the thorns from the earth and winds them into a new royal crown. Earthly wisdom is born out of earthly sorrow.

To know means to suffer. *This* crown is the picture of human kingship.

In ancient times there was seen around the head of wise men the glory of heaven, whose rays went up to the stars. Out of this in earliest time came the king's crown. This crown man has lost. He must weave for himself the new crown out of the thorns of the earth. Earth's pain must become wisdom. Every single pain has found its redemption, when it has become wisdom.

" I will stand before the world for that holy thing which is given to me ! I will expect nothing in return but thorns, but out of the thorns I will make a crown ! I will change all my earthly sorrow into humanly-divine wisdom ! " Not the appearance of holiness is sought by our new holiness, but the crown of thorns. We stamp into our souls the picture of Christ as He stands there, so that our ego may become like Him. And so the highest fidelity to God unites itself with the greatest clarity of mind concerning the earth.

One will find the meditation upon the crowning of thorns to be especially beneficial, because our age has in an especial way entered the earth and sought knowledge in it. Here is *the* human wisdom of the earth. We do not cherish a conception of life which sees in the earth only sorrows, and longs for heaven, but an attitude to life which changes the sorrows of earth into a crown. Nor do we cherish a view of the world which wishes to have a wisdom from heaven above, and despises the earth, but a will for the world which seeks and gathers divine wisdom in the sorrow of earth. Such a Christianity stands right between East and West, between the East, which seeks wisdom while it avoids the thorns of earth, and the West, which experiences the thorns of the earth without gaining wisdom from them. Here also man may come to drinking this wisdom with his ego like a draught from the Grail. But it is well that, while doing so, he should never lose from his soul the picture of the thorn-crowned Christ.

In Dr. Steiner's lectures it is told that the men of the Middle Ages, when they experienced the crowning with thorns, really felt sharp, pricking pains in the head. This is connected with the fact that in ancient times man saw the revelation of the circle of the stars before him as if in a ring round his head. The mitre still indicates that. For the word " Mithras " in the Persian religion, from which the " mitre " comes, means a " band " and is connected by learned men to-day with the light of the Zodiac. Now when man to-day feels the pains round his head, especially in the middle of his forehead, but not in it alone, also at the back of the head as if a ring were about to burst, then it may be a sign that he is again on the point of breaking through to divine wisdom. For this reason Christ appears in Revelation no longer with the crown of thorns, but with the light of the sun round his head. As in the feet a man's will can unite itself with the forces of the earth, as in the " middle of man " his life of feeling unites itself with the meaning of the cosmos, so in his head his spirit weds itself to wisdom, which has its spiritual home in the kingdom of the heaven of the fixed stars.

" Behold the man ! " says Pilate as he leads Christ out in his crown of thorns before the people. And our doubt, whether we can really find this saying significant, passes away when we learn that in the Persian mysteries the initiation proceeded in this way, that the man had to pass through a scourging, then received a royal mantle with a sceptre, but also with an acanthus crown. It is the same word acanthus as in the Bible account. The crown of thorns had a thorn in the middle of the forehead to indicate that the wisdom from sorrow must be conquered in the earthly ego which lives there. Previous to this point in the ceremony of initiation, as always in the mysteries, exercises in self-denial may have taken place, such as we see in the Washing of the Feet.

There is even a direct connection between these mysteries and the scene in Jerusalem. For in the Roman armies the service of Mithras was the favourite religion. When the soldiers heard that Christ was a king without a country, this scene was arranged out of mingled memories of the mysteries and scornful jests. The crown of thorns speaks only too clearly. Certainly the Persian Sakaean festival was then already well on its way to degeneration into the Roman Saturnalia.

Also the expression of Pilate, "Behold the man!" may have been a saying from the mysteries, that was really spoken on such an occasion when the initiation had come to an end. Pilate may have known this and have used the saying in a cynical sense. If this is so, then the saying of Pilate would become more explicable. More explicable also would be the wrath of the Jews which broke out just at this moment when, according to John's Gospel, they for the first time raised the cry : " Crucify him ! " for they either guessed or knew something about the background of the mysteries. At that time hardly any occurrence was to be thought of except in relation to such a background and the Jews naturally repudiated this entirely. In this sense also are to be understood the mystical experiences which, in the mediæval cloisters, as a necessity for life, were gone through in connection with the individual details of the story of the Passion.

We would, therefore, have this process of evolution before us. In the old mysteries, whose remains are still preserved for us in the Persian Sakaean feast, man was led out of Primal wisdom and inward knowledge of the laws of the cosmos to a consecration, but without Christ.

But they had a premonition of true humanity. In the Middle Ages they experienced Christ in deep sympathy but without knowledge of the secrets of the cosmos. Yet in their practice they penetrated to these secrets. Here in our exercises both are united. If the exercises are performed, not only in a sympathy with Christ which comes from the feelings, but with reference to their meaning for the world, then they can to-day take place upon a higher level of life.

It was again Rudolf Steiner who made clear the connection of the first stage of the Passion with the course of initiation into the Persian mysteries. We continue our thought, basing it upon what he has told us. In the details thereof, much may require confirmation, completion, perhaps also rearrangement; but what we actually see before us in the three pictures we have described is the evolving of a higher humanity. One can freely say, in the face of that which we have been considering, that the real qualities of men were not in existence before Christ, or only as in the mysteries, in a picture. Threefold is the world in which man stands. He lives among his fellow men : for this world Christ gives him love. He lives with his fate : for this world Christ gives him peace. He lives before God : for this world Christ gives him holiness. Behold the man !

It is not surprising now if in some readers the feeling arises that, simply because of all these meditations, he no longer knows upon what he ought to meditate. Let him think that we are here offering him aids for his whole life. If a reader at first stops short at the exercises for the ego, and reads everything else at first as a help to understanding the Bible, it is well. Even in this case the further amplification can be useful to him just exactly for these ego-meditations. He will see the direction in which it proceeds and find some detail important for his basic meditations, for example, the more exact description of love and peace.

Finally, we shall give suggestions as to how the whole organism of the twenty-one exercises can best be brought into corporate life. We should advise first holding fast the two fundamental meditations; from them proceeding further to attempt the ego-meditations, and from time to time the thorough reading of the exercises in the training of the will, which here begin : not merely reading them all through at once, as one reads a newspaper, but remaining at the pictures and allowing them to act upon one. One will thus be able also to come to a better method of reading the Bible. Whether one simply reads them now and again meditatively, or whether one is able, without neglecting the earlier meditations, to enter more strongly into the meditation of these pictures also; it is always advisable that one should actually feel, not so much the sorrows, as the *full humanity* of these pictures. It is the *real man* into whom we grow, when we " follow Christ." This man must be ready to take sorrows upon himself. Otherwise he cannot become a man upon the earth. But the sorrows are not what is essential. Deeply may we receive this into ourselves—what a glorious thought of God the man is who bears within himself royal love to all that is below him, heavenly peace towards all that is around him, and divine holiness before all that is above him. Then these three qualities must be purified, as they can be from the picture of Christ.

Through love man unites himself to earth. In peace he walks upon the earth. With the wisdom which is born from holiness, he turns from earth back to heaven. *Behold the man !*

VII

WHEN Pilate had spoken the words : " Behold the man ! " the priests and their servants answered with the cry : " Crucify Him ! " Such a scene, quite apart from its intense human interest, is full of world history.

There were then two ways of initiation, that of the North and that of the South. In the northern initiation—corresponding to the religion of the peoples to which this esoteric initiation belonged—the initiate was led more towards that which is outward, and experienced the meaning of the world. In the southern way of initiation, he was led into the depths of his own inward being and so broke through into the world's essential being. Of the northern way of initiation we have still got some inkling through that which is told of Persia. To the king of the Saturnalia, the proper festival which is connected with the Persian Sakaean Festival, two servants were given in later times, who clearly remind us of the thieves crucified on the right and left of Christ. The southern way of initiation, which found especially in Egypt its classic consummation, led the initiate through death to a resurrection. Often, the person to be initiated was even bound for three days to the Cross. We base our account of these occurrences upon the results of the spiritual investigations of Rudolf Steiner, which seem to us to be extremely probable. It must be left to others to examine the historical evidences, so far as these exist.

If these things are true, then in this scene before the judgment seat of Pilate, the South—naturally quite unconsciously or only little consciously—answers the North, out of the souls of the Jews. One might also say that humanity is saying to itself, " He has now reached the end of the northern way of initiation, He must also go the other way to the end," for the rites of initiation were not arbitrary customs, but corresponded to deep laws of the universe. If the northern way ended with Pilate's saying " Behold the man ! " the southern way must end with the saying " Behold the God ! " For he who goes through death to resurrection, passes over beyond humanity into the hosts of the supermen or gods, as the men of old times said. Thus the initiated in Egypt were addressed simply as Osiris. After the death of Christ we hear, for the first time from the mouth of the centurion of the cohort which crucified Him, the confession, " Truly this man was the Son of God." (Mark xv, 39.) And after the resurrection, Thomas makes the confession, " My Lord and my God ! " (John xx, 29.)

To-day it is necessary that we should reconquer for ourselves, in a new way, the Cross of Christ. Our studies will help to do this. We cannot have Christ without the Cross. But before we inwardly draw near to the most solemn picture in world history—" Christ on the Cross " —let us first answer some practical questions which arise when we meditate. One repeatedly hears the complaint that people, when they begin to meditate more strongly, feel disturbed by their own *breathing*. This sometimes arises from the fact that a man's breath becomes different when he gives himself up to intensive spiritual study. The breath becomes deeper, slower, healthier, purer. A man need do nothing to bring this about; it comes of itself. One then experiences at first hand how the " sickness of sin " has worked right into the body itself, and how through it, our breath also has become more shallow, more dead. Those who in a high degree have given themselves to worship, have a longer breath than others. One can feel this clearly in the rhythms of Bruckner's music, for example. And the incapacity, which even great conductors show when conducting Bruckner's music, is not seldom connected with their incapacity to experience the deep breathing of reverence which lives in Bruckner's works.

For men of to-day it is not right to begin the ascent to a more spiritual life by exercises in breathing. By very illuminating evidence Rudolf Steiner has proved that the Indian, as a " man of a rhythmic system," was especially capable of experiencing in his breath the divine, but that the European of the present day, being a " man of nerves and senses," has to tread another path. The Western man will never overtake the Indian upon his Indian way. It may, indeed, be said that in higher occult exercises a certain conscious and controlled drawing of the breath is a great help. The breath itself is also full of secrets, for it is much more living and spiritual than we, who are contemporaries of the age of materialism, know. But here it is enough for our purpose to know the following facts :—Meditation can also be practised as a conscious free dreaming. Wide awake and strong, guided by the will of man and illuminated by his consciousness, can that be accomplished, which happens in the dream—that we leave the corporeal and live in the spirit alone. Then one can easily come really to dreaming and lose oneself. But the breath—one can here speak only in pictures—may become for him a staff, by help of which he goes forward step by step. With each breath one fans the flame of complete consciousness, and in order not to pass out of free, conscious meditation into drowsy dreaming, he may even arrange that at every expiration the picture, which he wishes to place before him, represents itself to him actively and afresh, and that, in the same way, at every inspiration he draws the picture into himself, and lets it work strongly upon his whole being, as if he would

117

stamp it into himself, as if *it* would stamp *him*. And so he reaches a rhythm of inward experience, which assists him in keeping awake. Everyone whose breath troubles him may attempt this. Gradually he will come to need this help no longer. He will not need to trouble at all about his breath. Nor will he lose it, as often happens at the beginning. But after the meditation he will notice that he has been breathing beneficially. Then it will occur to him, in a healthy way, suited to the present time, why the men of past ages experienced the divine through breathing : the Jews again, in a quite different way from the Indians. In the New Testament the Holy Ghost too is brought into close connection with the breath of air, the human breath, pneuma. Christ breathed upon his disciples, as once God breathed into Adam, and said, "Receive ye the Holy Ghost."

But the following up of these truths would lead us too far away from our immediate goal. One can actually get as far as feeling that one is breathing in *the Holy Ghost*, that one has the impression that each breath one draws is laden with the Holy Ghost. This one can also perform as a meditation for oneself, without exercising the breath too severely. Everyone experiences the beginnings of such holy breathing in meditation.

Others assert that, in really strong meditation, disturbances in one's digestive system occur. In all such cases it is necessary to have calmness, and, if one may use the noble word—wisdom. Little disturbances are not harmful, and right themselves. If anyone thinks he has more serious difficulties, let him relax the strength of his meditation a little—until things are better. But I know concerning many people that, although they meditate as strongly as the body is able to bear, they suffer no harm from it. When once, at the beginning of strong meditation, I received the impression that the so-called lower man would not co-operate and coldness in the stomach set in, then Dr. Steiner said with perfect calmness : " Simply let some warmth flow to the stomach ! " I did so and the trouble passed off. A spiritual attitude which unites calmness, good sense and courage is the right attitude for meditation.

In our organism the many thousand years of sinfulness have brought about disorders which will be gradually put right again by meditation. Most people will notice scarcely anything of this. But let him who believes he perceives irregularities ask himself if these irregularities have not in this sense healthy after-effects. Perhaps he may find himself *so much the fresher* afterwards, although the meditation may have made his body suffer.

Some may find that they require to eat less when they meditate strongly. How much else occurs with regard to eating I have already discussed in connection with the saying " I am the Bread." But now people ask if vegetarianism does not heighten the power to meditate. One can only reply that it is better to put it the other way round ; that through right meditation one gradually becomes more of a vegetarian. Some people will never be able to become vegetarians, or, at least, not entirely so, because the bodies they have inherited will not allow them. They would faint if they tried to force them, for, owing to peculiarities in their constitution, they cannot produce the strength their organism would require in order to get from plant food the same nourishment as from meat. Here, also, one must have calm, sensible courage. Our organism, when we by meditation have acquired a more sensitive feeling for it, tells us exactly what we must do. If it itself refuses meat, then the hour has come when we may and can go over to vegetarianism. No further secret need or longing for meat will come to us. Then we need not trouble about medical theories that " the man " of to-day cannot live long without meat. Here, as in the case of the breath, the man of the present time can find through the spirit the right management of his body, whilst the man of past centuries rather approached the spirit through the right management of the body. There are men who would like " to eat their way into heaven," said Rudolf Steiner, in reference to some present-day movement. But it is a good thing when once we reach at least the first experiences of how meditation itself can feed men. As man can draw near in his breath to the Holy Ghost, so in his food he can draw near *to the Divine Son*. It is not by chance that the Lord's Supper is the principal religious worship of Christ.

In a third sphere, upon which we can merely touch here, man draws near to *the Father*. Not without deep meaning is the figure for the highest God, " the Father," taken from the human life-process itself. In regard to the sexual life, we can in this connection only say that here again one should train it through the spirit. Our studies in meditation would neglect an important duty and service if they did not tell young people that through strong, spiritual meditation, held with power in the soul, can help first come in a sphere, which, among people of the present day, is in a terribly bad condition. Right meditation brings to it successively order, purification, a calming influence and spiritualisation. It leads men, even if over a long period, on the way to becoming spirit. Where temptations occur, a quiet guiding away to the spirit is better and surer than violence. Our way is not that of unbridled asceticism. By this we do not mean that the helps often recommended, such as plain food, bodily exercise, moderate sleep, should be despised—not at all; we are thinking of other things. The wife need not be cold to her husband, as one often finds in women who, in a selfish way, wish to further their own " higher development," and who thus throw their husbands into bitterness against the spirit, or off the straight path. The earthly human faculties of love can be gradually raised to sharing in the divine creative will itself, without the commission of such errors. This creative will is indeed a divine will to sacrifice. The more naturally everything comes from the spirit itself and the less harshness that is necessary to ourselves and others, so much the better it is. Only the direct struggle for the pure, divine spirit cannot be sufficiently severe or earnest.

Christ on the Cross—that is the strongest picture on earth for meditation. If we would experience it anew to-day it is good first to look into the history of Christianity. There have been aberrations in two directions, and they will occur again and again. The first aberration is this, that one entered in thought into the sufferings of Christ in a way that was more personal and sentimental. The other aberration consisted in this, that one did indeed look at the outward event, but pushed it back into the past. The first error reached its climax in the mysticism of the Middle Ages. The second error came through the religiousness of the Protestants. In the first case we have, to use the language of spiritual science, a deflection towards the Luciferic side, towards the side of self-seeking. In the other case we have a deflection towards the side of Ahriman, towards the side of mental obscurity.

Certainly one ought at some time to represent to oneself the Crucifixion of Christ in all its terrible details, so that one may know the truth about how it happened. The throwing to the ground, the stretching out, the nailing of the hands and feet, the painful erecting of the Cross, the hanging by the wounds and their inflammation, the continuous dislocation of the body, the exposure to sun and insects, the torturing thirst, the bodily agony resulting from the painful position and the interrupted flagging circulation of the blood which resulted from it ; one has the impression that Christians have been very little conscious of the dreadful reality, and that almost without exception their pictures of the Cross, with the beautifully-carved wooden beams, and their hymns of the Cross, with their sentimental effusiveness in the face of that reality, do not in any case reveal that sincerity, compassion and reverence which we owe to the occurrence. He who has once let the Cross in its historical reality act upon him, feels as if he could never again in the future live as he has lived till now, as if an absolutely decisive happening had come to him, as if he were barred out, as it were, from his old life. A feeling comes over him which may be expressed in this way : " Upon the earth, where such a thing happened to Christ, I can never again seek artless joys. Towards humanity, which in its midst gave to Christ such a fate, I can only take up a standpoint on His side. In the world, in which such a sin against God is possible, I can only work with all my strength for a new world." This feeling about life, if we have once looked at Christ's death upon the Cross sincerely, is revived again as often as we think of the Cross. The Son of God—tortured fearfully to death by men—from the day when we have seen this, the world becomes different.

Some may think that in this experience everything is contained and that nothing more is necessary but to let it work itself out strongly. But that would be an experience which remained in the sphere of the soul and which would be no complete spiritual appropriation or penetration of that which happened then. And therefore it would appeal more to the feelings of an unspoiled soul, which is already near to Christianity, but would not contribute much to a spiritual understanding of the world—and would therefore not be strong enough ultimately to oppose the powers of the present time. The picture of Christ upon the Cross must not to-day be merely an impression upon the soul, however deep it may be, but must become an all-inclusive experience of the world, a last illumination of the world for us. Goethe's æsthetic distaste for the crucifix is also connected with this defect.

Here it is important to point out that, not only was the Cross no chance instrument of torture, but it was from the point of view of the mysteries, especially a picture of material existence. We recognise this when we remember the well-known passage in Plato's Timæus, in which this view of the mysteries is still apparent. In this is mentioned the world-soul, which is stretched in the form of a cross upon the body of the world. When, before the present stage of our earth's development, there was only a spiritual world, it was otherwise. Then the divine could be immediately present everywhere, as it still is to-day in the spirit. When the world was spread forth in the four spatial directions, this meant at the same time a decision for the divine, that it must allow itself to be spread out over the breadth of the world of sense. We are here speaking, in accordance with the senses, of four directions, that is to say, of a world of two dimensions, and are leaving out of consideration the third dimension, the direction upwards, because matter has within itself the tendency always to fall down from the upward direction when it can, and to spread itself out over the level ground.

This all sounds cold and abstract when we speak of it in the language of thought. But it may become a living experience. One then really feels the material world to be in the form of a cross on which God is outstretched.

In ancient times men have had a very strong feeling of such truths in a picture. Thus in the Vedas it is told how, when one reaches the inside of the world, one finds there the figure of a man who is fastened to a cross, on one side of him the sun, on the other the moon. *If God will have man to be what he can become upon earth, he must resolve to allow himself to be nailed to the Cross.* The usual Christian view to-day assumes too much "a chance historical occurrence," as Lessing said, and as the Indian critics still say. The Father of the World once resolved—that is more or less how one represents it to oneself—to redeem the world and to give His Son to death. From this humanity may judge how great His love is. If one looks at Church history, one will keep on finding men who have found a stumbling block to their feelings in such an act of the Father of the World, as it is described to them. They can be helped only when they see that Christ has simply revealed that which is itself the deepest fact of the world. The Father lives on the Cross in this earthly world of ours. He has formed the incredible resolve to stretch out His life over a shattered existence. All our life touches this fact of sacrifice. But Christ has raised up the Cross upon the earth as *the* divine revelation for all men. He has really raised it *up*. He has given it the direction towards the heights. In Plato the World Cross appears lying down. In Christ it stands. By this is pictorially expressed that the material existence is now finding its way upward again. The World Cross stands, since Christ, upright upon the earth.

From this viewpoint let us now look at man. He is built up in the form of a cross. Naturally this bodily form originated outwardly and historically, because man began to work about him with his hands and therefore had only his feet with which to stand upon the earth.

The law of the material form was in him, but already directed upward. And so we look with reverence at the upright posture of man. In it is announced before-hand, as in a prophecy, that man is destined to raise the earthly sense-existence upward again into the spirit. The power of erection, which has brought man from the horizontal into the perpendicular, is the same divine power, which in the fullness of time, has reared up the Cross to lead upward again.

Here also we must press forward from pale thought to full-blooded experience in life. If we again go through our fundamental meditation: I am Love! deriving it from Christ as strongly as we are able, and then look back again at our own body, and especially at its skeleton, we gradually acquire a really concrete idea from it of the way in which Christ is fastened to the Cross within us also. The German word "*Kreuz*" (Cross) for our back-bone acquires new meaning. In us Christ is cruci-fied—this is a feeling which actually expresses a very deep reality. The higher ego, in which Christ lives, bears the Cross in us as long as we live upon earth.

Certainly each of us has "his cross to bear" also in the sense that he has a hard fate to undergo. But that is not yet the Cross of Christ. Again, every man has to "take up his cross" if he will follow Christ, in the sense that through his standing up for Christ, for the Christ-conscience, for the Christ-ego within him, he brings sorrows upon himself, which he might have been spared. This comes nearer to the Cross of Christ. But we are "Crucified with Christ" in the full sense, when Christ lives so strongly in us that, every morning when we return into our body and into our earthly life, a new resolve is required to take our cross upon us, to let our-selves be fastened with Christ to the Cross. In this capital resolve are included all things that our fate may bring us. It is all-inclusive. Our personal fate becomes of no importance.

One cannot believe with what vividness the feeling of being crucified with Christ can fill a man. Down to the very details, one will experience the fact that every sacrifice of thoughts and feelings, which are connected with the sense existence, binds one more strongly to the Cross in one's being, makes one live more strongly in one's cross-form, yes, binds Christ in one ever and again to the Cross. But one will also experience that every stronger union with Christ makes one freer in respect of one's bodily existence, which lives in the Cross. Then Christ in one is less tied to the Cross, but freely bears the Cross. In such experiences one really becomes one with Christ and bears the Cross after Him. " If any man will come after me, let him deny himself, and take up his cross daily and follow me." (Luke ix, 23.)

Yes, the Cross will then become a living sign for us in all our daily experiences. In earlier times men made the sign of the Cross over that which they would dedicate to Christ. That has its own deep meaning and must be raised from being childish to being spiritual. We once discussed how every right practice of a profession, every true conversation, every earnest prayer is a passing through death to resurrection. But one can also experience how one's dying into one's profession can be a real stretching oneself out upon it, a permitting oneself to be fastened to it, in all its breadth and length, and therefore really being crucified. One's conduct of one's business becomes the better, the more one lays the Cross of Christ upon it, and gives oneself to the Cross. This resolve to allow ourselves to be fastened to the Cross must continually be taken in small things and in great. Thus life begins to take on the imprint of Christ. We may be able to do this only feebly as a beginner. But we learn also that a higher world has patience with us and helps us forward. What is necessary, is to be ever saying " yes " to Christ's royal sign upon earth—the Cross. This will to allow oneself to be stretched out and fastened to it must be ever renewed. *That is love.* The Father of the Worlds Himself is the Cross. One sees Him sometimes upon old crucifixes behind Christ. Out of the most high will of the Father of the Worlds this fact can reach into our daily lives. The more we live in this way, the better we understand Christianity. All that preceded this is but preparation. One can well understand that in this thought a greater Christianity is announced. In two directions Christianity becomes greater. The Cross of Christ is seen on the one hand in all its depths, and on the other it is carried into every single action. In this lies the germ of a new dogmatic as well as of a new ethic.

Buddha wished to overcome in his disciples the clinging to the earthly ; in Christ there follows the free fastening of oneself to the Cross of the world. We beg the reader not only to read these thoughts through once, but to let them come slowly to life within him. Ought one to leave them unspoken because they are still strange to many people to-day ? The deepest wisdom speaks from the Cross. Therefore it is the most powerful force in every-day life. It is a miracle which has given us the Cross. Christ has made the divine sign of the material world the symbol of love. Everywhere and always it is our duty to raise the Cross so that it points upward, to bring the earthly things of sense into the upward direction towards the heavenly. The Cross has magical power, as was dimly felt in ancient times. In it lives the will to the redemption of the world. " In this sign thou shalt conquer ! "

A man will also learn to treat his body quite differently

127

when he carries it as a cross. He may then feel like a crusader on whose back is the sign of the Cross. The mediæval crusaders were like the pictorial representation of a dim idea of what Christian men are. And so we may carry out the meditation upon the Cross in the following way. We place before ourselves Christ on the Cross, in entire historical accuracy as far as we can bear it. Then we let this picture grow spiritually greater, until it becomes the picture of the ultimate secret of the world, until we recognise that it is the revelation of the Father of the Worlds Himself, upon Whom our whole being depends. Then we let this picture impress itself upon us until we become it ourselves. We say " yes " to the fate which crucifies us with Christ, and make it our own will, our own act. We feel that this is the spirit of Christ's own love, which we must now carry into everything. Had we only the one direction, the direction outwards into the breadths of the world, we should lose ourselves through the world, as the *West* so often does. Had we only the other direction, the direction upwards to the heights, we should lose the world itself, as the *East* has so often done. It is just in the two directions of the Cross that we acknowledge the *ego in love*, that pours itself forth as widely as it raises itself, and raises itself as much as it pours itself forth. With all our strength we must spread out the ego in these two directions, and at the same time fill it with love. These two directions live also in the saying in which Christ sums up the Law and the Prophets—" Thou shalt love the Lord thy God with all thy heart, and with all thy soul and with all thy mind and thy neighbour as thyself ! " The ego feels itself to be a radiant cross, that from its safe centre strives away in two directions. Into that has matter changed itself. Many, to whom at first not all those cosmic thoughts mentioned above are certain truths, can carry out such meditations.

If, at the close of such a meditation, we cross ourselves outwardly also, we shall see that this action can bring us into full living fellowship with Christ.

Again the meditation upon the Cross is essentially strengthened, if we resolve to add to it the meditations which were known in the Middle Ages by the names "Mystic Death" and "Descent into Hell." Concerning these, Rudolf Steiner says in his Lectures upon St. John's Gospel : " Through the feelings which the pupil was made to experience at this stage, he experienced something which represented itself to him, as if in one moment a black curtain placed itself before all that was visible physically and as if everything disappeared. This moment is important also for another thing, which one must have experienced if one wishes to press forward really to Christian initiation in the true sense of the word.   One finds then that one can dive to the very bottom of evil, pain, misery and sorrow.   And one can taste to the full all the evil which exists in the depths of man's soul, when one descends into hell.   That is the ' Descent into Hell.'   If a man has experienced that, then it is as if the black curtain were rent asunder—and one looks into the spiritual world."

Here the mediæval experience is historically described. Only a few will be able to have it in this form to-day.   But it is not our task, nor is it the intention of Rudolf Steiner, to lead men into this experience in the way in which they once could enter into it.   That which was then reached by the way of the feelings, we must win again for ourselves out of our consciousness.   But a "Descent into Hell" belongs to the higher experience of the soul, to the higher training of the human ego for all time.   We already find such Descents into Hell in the pre-Christian mysteries.   In the tales of Heracles or of Odysseus, which actually represent inward experiences of initiation

129

in a popular form, we find a " descent into the under-world." It is especially instructive to follow the transformation of this primal experience of humanity in the new age. When Luther sings :

> And were the world all devils o'er
> And watching to devour us,

a kind of Descent into Hell glimmers out, in the shape of an experience in our consciousness. Carlyle tells of something similar about himself, under the name of Professor Teufelsdroek : " 'What *art* thou afraid of ? Wherefore, like a coward, dost thou forever pip and whimper and go cowering and trembling ? Despicable biped ! What is the sum-total of the worst that lies before thee ? Death ? Well death : and say the pangs of Tophet too, and all that the Devil and Man may, will or can do against thee ! Hast thou not a heart ; canst thou not suffer, whatsoever it be and, as a Child of Freedom, though outcast, trample Tophet itself under thy feet, while it consumes thee ? Let it come then ; I will meet it and defy it ! ' And as I so thought, there rushed like a stream of fire over my whole soul and I shook base Fear away from me for ever. I was strong, of unknown strength, a spirit, almost a god. Ever from that time, the temper of my misery was changed, not Fear or whining sorrow was it, but Indignation and grim, fire-eyed Defiance. Thus had the Everlasting No pealed authoritatively through all the recesses of my being, of my ME, and then it was that my whole ME stood up in native, God-created majesty and with emphasis recorded its Protest. Such a Protest, the most important transaction in Life, may that same Indignation and Defiance in a psychological point of view, be fitly called. The Everlasting No had said ' Behold, thou art fatherless, outcast, and the Universe is mine ! ' (the devil's) ; to which my whole ME now made answer: 'I am not thine, but Free and forever hate thee!' It is from this hour that I incline to date my Spiritual New-birth or Baphometic Fire-baptism : perhaps I directly thereupon began to be a Man." (Sartor Resartus Bk. II, Ch. VII, end). Such accounts are evidences of how certain inward experiences of the soul return of inner necessity and how they are transformed. Many similar examples could be found.

But is not " Christ's Descent into Hell " a legendary picture, which has nothing to do with the Gospels ? We need not join battle with such representations and we bring against them only Christ's saying : " Hereafter I will not talk much with you ; for the Prince of this world cometh, and hath nothing in me." (John xiv, 30.) Out of such a fundamental frame of mind has Christ on the Cross prayed : " Father, forgive them, for they know not what they do ! " Such a frame of mind is sufficient foundation for our meditation.

It is of the greatest importance, if we look closely at it, that behind the evil in the world, there are powerful spiritual forces which have taken up arms against the goal of the earth, which is Christ. In our times it is often as if we must come up against this fact violently. Paul also experienced that " we wrestle not against flesh and blood, but against principalities, against powers, against the rulers of the darkness of this world, against spiritual wickedness in high places." (Eph. vi, 12.) Such a point of view makes us lenient towards men. We understand that they are agents in the service of powers whom they themselves do not recognise. We learn to separate them from that which works in them. And we acquire the right will to redeem, the wish to " save," of which the Bible speaks so often.

And as this consideration gives us the real helper's frame of mind towards men, it also brings us fully into the seriousness of the world's situation. There are really, as we see them represented in pictures of the Catalaunian battle, according to old visions, spiritual armies above us, fighting for the earth. Many devilries which happen would not be understood by us if we did not know that here more than human intelligence, and more than human will is working through men. To win the victory, our own strength could never be enough. But when the victory is won by Christ also, as we can indeed inwardly feel, then we wage the fight with all our strength, " He will keep the field." To fight with Christ against hell means to stand on the alert in the fight for the world. But then one must see hell. The earth is a stage of a terrible struggle between light and darkness.

Here Dürer's picture can be a help—" The Christian Knight who rides on between Death and the Devil." A better help is Rudolf Steiner's statue of Christ, where, under the benignant, upraised left hand of Christ, Lucifer, the self-seeking power, dashes himself down into the depths, and where, under the spiritually powerful right hand, which is being uplifted, Ahriman, the earthly, sensual power sinks into the abyss. Faust saw Mephistopheles and sought to make him subservient. What we need is something still greater. We redeem the evil powers themselves when we, in the service of the world, prove ourselves unconquerable by them.

If we wish to seek for an inner exercise to this end, it may be connected with the Cross upon Golgotha. The sun ceases to shine : it is night. Nothing but night surrounds the Cross ; and this night is not only an outward night ; supremely powerful forces surround the Cross. But the Cross stands in light, still and strong. As a mighty sign of God it towers into the darkness. The upright Cross points straight up to the heights. Invincibly, there is revealed in it the power which opposes to all the might of the downward-drawing

forces the power that draws upwards. He who holds
strongly in this world to this direction, overcomes
Ahriman. The cross-beam of the Cross points into the
widths of space. It stretches itself fearlessly into the
darkness. In it is announced the power which opposes
to all the forces which strive away from the earth—the
power of blessing. He who bears this direction within
himself overcomes Lucifer. We see Christ shining upon
the Cross. He is the new light of the sun which van-
quishes all darkness. If our own spirit cannot penetrate
all the darkness around us, yet our ego in Christ is
stronger than it. We make the vow—let come what may :
let innumerable hosts of the forces of the adversary come
against me, and seek to destroy me ; I unite my ego to
Christ, Who shines upon the Cross. In Him I am conqueror. An unassailable peace from God fills the soul
in the face of all that threatens us.

So upon a higher, super-personal, cosmic level we
again acquire that which we acquired in the meditation
upon the scourging—peace. And we have acquired
again in the meditation upon the Cross on a higher
super-personal, cosmic level what the meditation upon
the Washing of the Feet gave us : Love becomes now
great as the world and peace deep as the world. A higher
greatness is not possible. After this experience follows
the resurrection. It brings, upon a higher, super-
personal, cosmic level the same as the meditation upon
the Crowning with Thorns : the holiness which is spread
out over the world.

When we unite the resolve to love with the meditation
on the Cross, and the victorious power of peace with the
meditation on the Descent into Hell, when we see the
Cross like a sign from Heaven, which God Himself
plants in the darkness of earth, when, in this sense we lay
hold of our task upon earth anew and freely, we can

crown this two-fold meditation with the words of the Act of Consecration of Man :

> For on the Cross will the body bear the new confession.
> And from the Cross in the blood will flow the new faith.

Our confession of Christ is the strength which directs our life upwards. Our faith in Christ points us to the world again. The disciple of Christ is just as much raised above the world as he is devoted to it in sacrifice. The Cross is the sign of Christ, as the wheel is the sign of Buddha. The wheel stands for the doctrine of the self-redemption of man. The Cross speaks of self-sacrifice for the redemption of the world.

Finally, our meditation will pass over into a communion. This may happen in every meditation, but here with especial force. The body in which Christ lived was in itself already the upraising of the earth towards Heaven. In Him lived and worked all the forces which draw the sense-being upwards. When we unite ourselves to this upward-directing power of Christ, those powers enter our body which make it like to Christ. We receive from the Christ-forces a new body, which itself is in a comprehensive way " the new confession " and the victory over Ahriman. And when, in this new body, we feel the stream of love, the power of sacrifice which pours itself abroad, then we become *one blood* with Christ. And this is, in the ultimate divine sense, " the new faith " and the victory over Lucifer. One can actually feel oneself as a cross shining in the darkness, and all the powers of God united in one. Only when Christ is in us can that truly happen. He holds us, as He Himself is held in old pictures and on old crucifixes by the Father, to the Cross. A mighty strength proceeds from such a meditation.

It is not that ultimately we "believe in the Cross," but that we become the Cross. In its earthly existence our life can bear no other character. With full consciousness we place ourselves in the world as a cross upon which Christ shines and conquers. He who has been with Christ upon the Cross—and this which we seek to arouse by meditation may also happen without clear consciousness of it—can hope to rise again with Him. "Follow me!" said Christ, and by that He did not mean the "life of poverty" nor chiefly the "going into all the world," but just the Cross. Behind the Cross, behind it alone, waits the resurrection.

In the words of a poet we can let what we have discussed ring out, and penetrate all our thoughts with strong feeling. Christian Morgenstern says—

The deepest secrets of the human form I've seen
    I know this world and that on which 'tis based,
I know that love, yea, love is what they mean,
    And that to love I here on earth am placed.
I stretch my arms out wide as He has done of old,
    I would that I, like Him, might all the world
        enfold.

VIII

WHEN we were students, the now nearly forgotten philosopher, Class gave us a simple key to the study of works of art, which may be of service to others. We should let each work of art act upon us for a time as a whole, and then look at all its details, and lastly, take it into ourselves as a whole once more, full of all the impressions it has made upon us.

This advice is not unsuited to meditation. In meditation one withdraws oneself into some saying or picture. One lets it be there and act upon one as strongly as possible. When one shuts one's eyes, one can almost fill the whole space in which one is living quite full with the content of the meditation, so that nothing else is present in it. Then we begin to notice how meditation works right into the delicate substratum of our bodily organisation, how it forms our hidden life forces in its own image. Every meditation actually forms within us new life forces. Just as Rudolf Steiner could describe how every medicine, as it were, fills a man ; that, for example, if a man regularly take mercury, one can perceive spiritually in him a delicate man of mercury, which grows stronger and stronger, just so is it with the spiritual medicine— meditation. And here also, in every powerfully accomplished meditation, the action becomes stronger, and several meditations can act very favourably in supplementing one another. If the meditation be strongly carried out, it may even cause bodily pains, because the new thing, which wishes to enter into us, comes up against the old. But these pains are not like other pains.

136

They are rather healing pains than pains of sickness, and leave behind them when they cease—and this is in our own hands—a feeling that one has become well again. Yet one need not pay attention to the pains, but only to the picture, the saying, the spirit. If the first stage of its consideration has been made as powerful as one can make it, one may then let the details of the picture, or of the saying, act upon one. In such a saying one feels oneself to be in a temple, at which one looks in all its details without ever leaving it. Thus, in the meditation upon the Cross, one can first consider the one direction and then the other; first the Cross itself and then Christ upon the Cross. One's efforts are directed always towards letting everything act as strongly and as long as possible. One may repeat one's study of the successive details several times, if one is not yet able to remain as long as one would like over one impression. Then, in the third stage of the meditation, one will have the entire meditation more strongly, more clearly and more richly alive in one's soul.

Such advice does not give essential conditions of meditation. It is only the reporting of experience, in order to help or arouse. In every case, however, it is good at the end of a meditation to bring its results clearly to one's consciousness, and to let them re-echo within one in all completeness.

Now there are many people who do not at first succeed in staying within a picture, as it were, or within a saying and living in it. For those it is especially good if they repeatedly go through the simplest of exercises in con-centration, in the form in which Rudolf Steiner has given it. One chooses some trifling object—a pencil, a pin, a ring. And then for five or ten minutes one forms only such thoughts as refer to this object. One may think successively of the shape of the pencil, of its colour, of its making, of its use. One always brings the thought, however simple it is, to the greatest possible clearness and strength, holds it for a moment in full consciousness, and then passes over freely to the next thought. It is not at all necessary that the thoughts should be weighty. On the contrary, the more trifling the object, the more everyday the thoughts, the more must a man call up freely from his own will the power to shape them and to hold them fast. And that is better for spiritual training than if a man, through the interest which flows into him from the object, should be driven on of himself. " This pencil is eight inches long—three-eighths of an inch in diameter— it is octagonal in shape—it might also be round—in that case it would have such an appearance—it consists of two pieces of wood stuck together—between them is graphite —it is brown—it might be blue—it was made . . . ." One may go through these thoughts successively and also in the reverse order.

An exceptionally beneficial feeling spreads itself over the whole brain, when one performs such a meditation strongly. One feels as if, for the first time, one were beginning to be master in one's own house. The king-liness of free thinking begins to be experienced. One begins to control oneself much more, to notice much more in other forms of spiritual activity where it is that one goes spiritually astray, to feel much healthier in one's attitude to life. I have known people who, after such an exercise, dreamt next night that they could ride beauti-fully. And indeed, to dream of horses not infrequently points to experiences in the sphere of thought, as for ex-ample, when we dream of galloping horses because our nerves are upset. Just as quite simple finger-exercises enable the artist to control quite differently the instrument upon which he afterwards plays a sonata, so it is with such a short mental exercise. In my own case, although

I rightly believed that I could work concentratedly, this simple exercise has enabled me to shorten by half my preparation for a lecture, not only because one becomes much clearer and more alert, but above all because one notices much more clearly the moments when one's mind is not upon one's work.

When the child rears itself upright, it learns first to walk freely and afterwards to stand freely. And so it is organically correct that one should first learn to move on in thought, before one can stand still in thought. And this simple exercise in concentration can be of great value to everyone, up to the greatest thinkers. Many a university professor, who looks down smilingly upon such an exercise with a pencil as mere childishness, would cease to laugh after four weeks and would notice that the five minutes spent daily upon it, would save him very much time and labour. In all activity this exercise is helpful, and for the nerves it is very especially healthy.

In this exercise itself, which we here allude to as preparatory to our meditations, there lies exceptional power to make one stand upright. It is not by chance that we mention it now, when we wish to speak of Christ's resurrection. One may know how to say the very noblest things about Christ's resurrection and may yet be able to see clearly the connection between the resurrection and such an exercise which is performed in the spirit, out of the free ego. Just that one should see these two together is a sign that one's attitude to life is quite natural.

To-day, certainly, there are not a few among those who feel themselves responsible for the life of mankind, and who wish to work for inward training among wide circles, who would advise directly against such a method of caring for the inner life as is here advised. The arguments which are brought against it are so characteristic and so numerous that we shall touch upon them.

139

Some think, for example, that one should not create for oneself quiet hours out of one's work time, but should note where *in* the work itself moments for self-recollection come. And one should then consider, not any particular saying from any particular book, but the thoughts which the work itself brings. All this may certainly bring blessing, and for a thinker or author it might be sufficient. But a workman or housekeeper would not find it enough. The result of this advice would be that one would neglect regular morning prayer and wait to see if some time during the day an impulse to prayer came. Similarly, Johannes Müller has said that prayer is quite real only when it is the natural answer to a divine revelation given to us. The further result of this would be that one no longer had any special place or time for divine worship, since one might have divine worship at any time in any place, and everything ought to grow out of life " quite naturally."

In truth there shows itself here the same over-valuing of the outward life as against the inward life, and the same over-valuing of impulses which come from without, as against the will which works from within, which we regard as a danger ; yes, as exactly *the* danger of our time, which, because mankind will be ruined by it, we are engaged in combating by our studies in meditation. If we admit as valid only the thoughts which come to us of themselves in our work, in our lives, these thoughts will, in the case of most people, be very poverty-stricken. It would be a very great loss and a strange folly, if we should neglect all that humanity has acquired in the course of its great spiritual history. But we can, of our own free will, place these great achievements in human history in the centre of our mind and receive them into ourselves more thoroughly than is possible by cursory reading, or hearing, or thinking. It would be entirely one-sided if we

140

allowed ourselves to be led by life only from without and gave no heed to that which can lead us from within. But to the inward possibilities belongs that of being able to recognise spiritual laws under which we can place ourselves, as, for example, the law of the morning hour, of rhythm, of repetition, that we can experience the power of special hours of consecration, that we should have a will through which we are able to turn of our own accord, freely, to the higher world. Prayer also, even when it is primarily the answer to a revelation, can then, as a free act, without hindrance from without, rise out of that which is within.

Certainly all this may happen unnaturally, may be laboured and forced. And from the fact of these dangers, such warnings acquire a certain power to root themselves firmly in men's souls. Yet at their root lies a defective experience of the hidden spiritual laws, and a defective consciousness of the necessity of working to-day, more than formerly, from within outward, and, above all, of placing the will in the service of the spirit. So the enemies of progress are extreme individualism, as Protestant religiousness has trained it, passivity in the religious life, as it has been handed down to us from the past, and materialism, which does not oppose strongly enough the inward to the outward life.

But progress consists in the perception that the spiritual life has its own special laws and possibilities, upon which one does not stumble of oneself in everyday life, that only a very assiduous nurture of one's inward powers will save us from ruin and that at the present time free will must above all be awakened and made the vehicle of the Divine. The higher man ascends, the more the outward guidance by life is replaced by the inward guidance, the higher ego, which derives its aims and its laws from the spirit.

141

This is above all true of the resurrection, which we must to-day make our own in a new sense. To men in earlier times was brought simply the message of Christ's resurrection. That worked immediately upon their life of feeling and of will. Now, on the one hand, the certainty of the Biblical proclamation has been shattered. Men bring their doubts against the Biblical account and its historical accuracy. On the other hand, the connection between conception, feeling and will is no longer so living and immediate in men. Many more hindrances are to be overcome. We must work at the highest which is in us more consciously and with stronger will-power than did men of past ages.

He who wishes to experience the resurrection in a living way within, may start from feeling the earth to be a great grave. It is. The very earth upon which we walk is a graveyard. Everywhere beneath us are corpses of living things which have died. The earth is pervaded by decaying plant life. The sand itself is rock crumbled and broken down. And if it should be, as anthroposophical spiritual science says, that the world of stars at which we gaze is seen by us as physical only because we are physical men, but that they are in reality much more spiritual and do not consist of perishable matter, then one might almost say : In the cosmos, the earth is the great grave. That which lives on earth must die. One will have the right feeling about the earth if one brings this into one's full consciousness. Every individual thing which we see bears within it the sign of death. It is often startling when, after some years, one sees an acquaintance again and perceives clearly how death has put its mark upon his face. Death can be seen everywhere, only our eyes are still but little open to it. One may make it an inner exercise to represent to oneself those people whom one sees now in the prime of life,

and to say to oneself : In 100 years, there will remain of
you, as I now see you before me, only a few bones in a
coffin. It is said that once, in Nuremberg, a preaching
monk, John a Capistrano, said from the pulpit—" Would
you like to know how you will look in 100 years ? "
And, as all eyes were raised to the pulpit, he brought
out a skull from under the desk, held it up and said,
" Thus ! " Of all the sermons of all the preachers who
had preached in the Church of the Holy Ghost at
Nuremberg throughout the centuries, only this one was
actually remembered when I was pastor there. We are
doing nothing extraordinary, nothing ascetic, but we
are seeing the truth, when we bring our capacity to see
death, which is ruler of this world, much more strongly
to life within us, than it is present to our superficial
and fundamentally cowardly age.

Everything around us is dying—the people, trees,
mountains, civilisations, this planet itself. Buddha was
more logical than the people of the present day when he
wished to have this truth ever before his eyes. Buddha
may for ever help humanity to see the great grave—in which
the resurrection must follow ! If Christ were not, then
Buddha would have the ultimate truth.

If we have succeeded in gaining this sight with perfect
clearness—the earth is the great grave—then we must
look up to Christ. It is possible to look simply at the
Risen One. Then one looks into a world of light
which is of quite another kind than the world which is
passing away, which otherwise we have around us.
Every touch of this world brings awakening and life
triumphant over death. Doubt is quite impossible if
Christ is really there. He is the resurrection and *the* life.

As long as we are not permitted this look, we must
give heed to the life which we feel to be in Christ, to
the life which through Him is awakened in us. We

143

must not be too soon disappointed, but must observe and wait, until we, in the words of the Apostle Paul, " know Him and the power of His resurrection." We must truly experience how different He is from this passing world here ; how, in Him the eternal, which is above time, is revealed. It is merely a matter of the power of our spirit that we should see the victory over death which is in Him. I wish we could name some picture of the resurrection in which the Risen One is convincingly revealed. I know of none, not even Grünewald. So we may let the saying, " I am the Resurrection and the Life," pass through our souls, and may feel especially the power of the light in this ego so vividly, that in it we pass beyond death. The resurrection of Christ must be experienced to-day in its own peculiar essence, if we are to be able to believe in that resurrection in the past, must be experienced not as a joy in one's soul, but as a cosmic act. Let him, who does not yet feel Christ, look upon his own higher ego, as far as he feels it, or upon the good. Even he who is at first sure of nothing but the wish, " I will serve the good even if I myself am lost," even he feels a beginning of the resurrection.

Now that we have thought of the great world, let us think of ourselves also. Our body is a grave. Some day we shall throw it aside like a husk that has become use-less. Then we give up, not the spirit, but the body. Many men have felt that one ought never to conceal this truth by living happily in one's body, that one ought to bring it clearly into one's consciousness, that without this consciousness one can by no means be a man or live as a man in the true sense. And so, like some monks of the Middle Ages, they have slept in their coffins in order to remind themselves daily of death. Or, like the Protestant, August Hermann Francke, they have represented to themselves every evening as they went to sleep, that this might have been their last day, and every morning as they awoke, that they had received one single day more to be spent in honouring God. August Hermann Francke confessed that he owed his life to this custom. That also was a meditation that showed its power in this way.

We may feel the traces of decay in our body. Perhaps we already know the spot where death has lodged itself and out of which it can one day fall upon us, and destroy us. We consider all this with great calm. As calmly as, at the end of his " Monologues," Schleiermacher addresses the white hair which begins to appear upon his head and as Fichte in his " Mood of a Scholar " speaks of the extinction of the last speck of sun-dust in his body.

These are not pessimistic reflections, or sentimental self-complacencies, or ascetic torturings of the soul, but natural preparations for experiencing the resurrection powerfully. One may, before going to sleep, or after awaking, propose this question as an exercise for the soul : " What would remain of thee if thou hadst no longer a body ? " Then, of course, the body must be quite at rest, so that it no longer is a part of one's experience. Then the outer world must be completely silent, so that it does not lay hold of or disturb our consciousness. Then all thoughts and feelings which thrust themselves up out of our bodily life into our spirit must be left behind. Some will find it hard then, especially, still to lay hold of and hold fast to anything. They may then form for themselves the idea that it is not so easy to awake in a spiritual world after death, and that difficulties must then be overcome, and the more materially one has lived, the more there will be of them—even if, after the falling away of the body, helps are there for us. If a man, who seeks to conceive of himself apart from his body, at first is able to hold fast to nothing, or only to something quite thin and flickering, let him then think of Christ. He will then be able to experience quite strongly how he is filled from within with the riches of glowing life, how this life has especially the character of being spiritually steadfast, enduring, sustaining. And so he will experience quite intimately and personally something of an awakening through Christ.

It is powerfully and entirely convincing to know from one's own experience how Christ breathes into the dry bones, how through Him a new life is lent to men.

And now one will confess : this is also the true holiness in my everyday life, that I should in all things confess Christ, who fans the flame of a higher life within me. That which I have experienced on a more human level, in the crowning with thorns, I here experience in cosmic super-human greatness. In John's Gospel it is often said of the " word " of Christ that it awakes man, gives him eternal life (*e.g.* in the sixth chapter). We now experience this as if Christ Himself were the Creative Word spoken by God, through which we are again created out of death. Yes, one may experience this as if we ourselves were quite dead, and out of deep invisible grounds of the world, in which the Divine Father lives, Christ's word of life is spoken ; and as if we awake in Him to life, to new life, to real life. We take all the wisdom and holiness, which will henceforth lead us in life, out of this living Christ. In the " Act of Consecration of Man " it says : " O Christ, I confess unto that which is revealed through Thee ; the might of man's adversary Thou takest from me."

If Christ's word of life is not strong enough to bring about in us such a resurrection, which is only a first pale gleam of the real resurrection, a great help may be— scarcely indeed any painting that exists to-day—but the living picture of the Risen Christ given in the Bible.

The Risen Christ appears in three ways in the New Testament. He appears first in the way in which He reveals Himself to the disciples between Easter and Ascension. Here John's Gospel is especially important. It tells us most circumstantially and impressively of the Risen One. No one ought to let the seasons of Easter and Whitsuntide pass without letting these accounts act upon him. Over them is spread a fragrance and beauty, as of spring in Elysium. To breathe this spirit of the resurrection in these stories awakes a man himself to a new life.

A second kind of resurrection occurrence is described in that which happened at Damascus, when Paul met the Risen One. We have earlier indicated the organic connection of this appearance with the experience at the baptism in Jordan and with the revelation to Stephen. All these can help us if we wish to reach an impression of the Risen One. These stories are meant for that purpose.

But here, for our meditation, we would point especially to the last and greatest revelation of the Risen Christ in the Apocalypse of John (Rev. i). As nowhere else we can really get to know the Risen One in this picture, live ourselves into Him, and thus ourselves arise. This picture is the most powerful meditation upon the resurrection.

Step by step we can call this Christ up before us, and if at first the picture is strange to us, because we study such pictures from a too outward, too materialistically painted standpoint, are too little able to read and bring to life within us the language of the spirit which is spoken there, we must let such pictures become more living and vivid than we are accustomed to receive pictures to-day : then we live ourselves ever more strongly into them.

The head shining in pure light, as if itself created out of purest light, wisdom and holiness in one ! Out of it

the eyes shine forth, " as the sun shineth in his strength."
Thus the head is surrounded from without with cosmic
divine light and at the same time—in the eyes—filled
from within with the essence of divine light: outward and
inward meet.

The garment with the golden girdle is the same that
we have recognised in these studies as divine peace, the
divine support which proceeds from super-earthly cosmic
harmony. That this peace is no rest apart, but the
strongest cosmic force, we recognise from the voice
which comes forth from the breast, which is as the rushing
of mighty waters ; which acts like a two-edged sword of
judgment. Again we see this peace more inwardly in the
garment with the golden girdle, and more directed towards
the world in the mighty cosmic word.

And the love of which we first spoke is shown in the
picture to us in the feet, which are formed out of earth-
force, out of brass, but heavenly fire glows through them
and in the hands, in which live the powers of the stars.
Again, a more personal side of love is depicted in the
feet, and the side turned towards the world is depicted in
the hands.

John the Seer tells us of himself that, when he had seen
this Christ, he fell to earth as one dead. We always
appear dead near Him. We experience the great grave,
the earthly world, and the little grave, our earthly body.
The greatest person before Christ, Buddha, is fully in our
consciousness within such a study. Thus we look upon
Christ and receive out of Him true humanity. Yes, we
can now see, summed up in this Christ, the whole construction of these our exercises in life, as far as they refer
to character. That which is brought about through the
foot-washing we see here in the earthly feet, through which
the fire glows—earth power united to the spirit of love.
That which the *scourging* brought, comes back in per-

fection in the flowing garment with the golden girdle. That which the *crowning with thorns* awoke in us, the standing for that which is sacred in us, earthly life raised to heavenly wisdom, shines forth from the eyes ; in the noblest thing which the earth can bring forth, in the human eye, shines the power of the sun itself. And now follow the three higher exercises also. That to which the *Cross* led us, the becoming one with cosmic love, lives as creative power in the pierced hands which hold the stars. The last judgment of the world into which *the descent into hell* led us, lives in might in the divine voice. And the *resurrection* itself, the awakening to a new being, is woven around the head as a heavenly fullness of light. We may think of these details, or have the whole before us : this is the Risen One, as He appeared to His beloved disciple ! So He would draw all men up to Him. Before Him all prayer becomes worship.

Where to-day is a pure worship of Christ to be found ? It would be the noblest prayer. Through Christ, we worship the World-Father " in Christ's name." What might not humanity become if the picture of the Risen One did not remain in the grave of the Bible, but arose in souls themselves ? What unheard-of development would men bring forth from within ? With deepest reverence, man, as he is, would look towards man, as he ought to become. He shines forth from Christ as the " Divine Son."

Let him who cannot yet honestly connect this picture of Revelation with a Christ alive to-day, think of it all at first as his own higher ego, or as the ideal for man. One day it will become clear to him, that he has there before him not only a thought picture of his own making.

With all this we are now already in the midst of the *Ascension.* One feels the whole contradiction of our time, when one merely speaks this word. Men who live among machines, ought they to sink themselves into the resurrection of Christ? But from quite another side comes a consideration. We read in the before-mentioned lectures of Rudolf Steiner on the Gospel of John " The seventh feeling cannot be expressed in words : he alone could describe it, who was able to think without using the instrument of the human brain ; and for this there is no language, because our language has expressions only for the physical plane. Therefore one can only give indication at this level. It surpasses all which man can represent to himself. One calls it the ' ascent into heaven,' or ' the complete absorption into the spiritual world.' "

According to such words we shall retain in our consciousness that there are experiences which lie high above all that we are able personally to reach. It is good in our last meditation to carry this quite clearly in our soul. And yet we must not pass by the highest. Not only because to the descent into hell of which we speak, an ascent into heaven alone can bring the balancing compensation, if we wish to have all correctly balanced— just as the death on the Cross corresponds to the resurrection—but because it is just the man of the present day who must come to feel again most strongly that he belongs to the divine world, if he is to oppose to the strong outward life the strongest contrary force.

Here also we shall walk most surely and may be protected from all dangers, if we follow the indications of the Bible itself.

Immediately before His Ascension, Christ instituted Baptism : " Make disciples of all nations, baptising them in the name of the Father and of the Son and of the Holy Ghost ! " Baptism, also, may be experienced on the most differing levels. When, starting from the picture of Christ which we have described, a man seeks to mount personally to where he plunges his whole thinking, the whole being of his head, into the Holy Ghost, to where he plunges his whole feeling, his whole " middle man " which lives in heart and blood and lungs, into the Divine Son, to where he plunges his whole will, which lives in our acts and in our walk, into the Divine Father, then he mounts into the region where man himself is an image of the Divine Trinity ; then the thrice holy Divine Name, which is above all the heavens, echoes wonderfully in man, then he becomes *one* with the life of the primal Divinity, which rules all the worlds and is raised above all the powers of evil, then he is in his highest heavenly father-land. Like a victor, crowned with light, he returns back to his earthly tasks. All the heavens are gathered within him and yet holier heavens will open to him in prospect. A man can seem to himself to be trans-figured in heaven. But he must not sink down into unconsciousness, which was the danger of the mystics, but in his awakened ego the heavens themselves will awake. It is the highest perfection of man, which we build up above the child in a sacramental action when we baptise it. Nothing must be in my thinking, but that which is the Holy Ghost ! Nothing must live in my feeling, but that which is the Divine Son ! Nothing must act in my will, but that which is the will of the Father of the world, Who is over all that exists ! One can ex-perience this meditation as a sealing with a divine seal.

Such a meditation will sanctify us, as nothing else can sanctify us. To have been in heaven—that gives one for life quite a different feeling towards the earth. Divinely ennobled we come back to it. But that is only possible when we have not sought to escape the Cross and hell. If we have received the divine seal, we learn to speak the word " man " in quite a different way. We begin to feel that man himself is called to enter the ranks of the divine beings, and to feel what *his* being, when among them, will be in light, life and love. For these three words of John's Gospel express the same thought, " Is it not written : Ye are Gods ? " (John x, 34.) Behold the Man ! Behold the God !

But the Ascension, if we do not deny the spirit of Christ, must never betray us into wishing to remain in heaven, however strongly we should feel it as " blessedness." The will of Christ leads straight from heaven to earth ! Only then are we united to Christ, if this will itself is alive in us also.

Thus indeed it was at the Baptism of Christ Himself. It can be regarded as an actual ascent to heaven. The connection between the Ascension and Baptism, as we described it above, becomes in it fully clear. And so the consideration of the Baptism of Christ can help us to strengthen the meditation upon the Ascension by means of a picture drawn from the earth.

" The heavens were opened." This experience of Jesus at the Baptism in Jordan, was, as Rudolf Steiner says, the deepest experience that ever a man had upon the earth. In the bright dove which lighted upon His head, the Holy Ghost revealed itself. In the voice which sounded, " Thou art my well beloved Son, upon whom my revelation rests lovingly," the Divine Son is revealed.

In the opening of the heavens over Him and around Him, the Father of the worlds drew near. That which we here see before us, was a passing through the three realms : Imagination, in the picture ; Inspiration, in the sound; Intuition, in the receiving of life. By this event— the Baptism of Christ—our ascent to heaven may at the same time be anchored and remain fast held within the realm of earth. We will also remind ourselves how Christ returned back after His Baptism into earthly life and after the temptation in the wilderness—the severest temptations often come directly after the highest experiences—the humdrum activities of daily life began, through which thereafter the kingdom of heaven glowed from the background. "The kingdom of Heaven is at hand!" was henceforth His announcement. When through our earthly activities also there shines a kingdom of heaven in which we have been, then they contain their real beauty and true grandeur.

Resurrection and Ascension complete one another like breathing in and breathing out. The Resurrection is a going into heaven. The Ascension becomes a returning from heaven. The two belong together as the highest communion. The Resurrection is a last receiving of Christ's body. The Ascension fills us in the deepest sense with Christ's blood. The Lord's Supper is the preparation for this experience.

If we look back upon the whole course of the purification of our feeling, we find that we have twice passed through the realm of love, of peace, of holiness. Like a spiral movement our way proceeded upwards, since the second circuit lay above the first. Into love, which is our relationship to our fellow-men, into peace, which is our relationship to the earthly world around, into holiness, which is our relationship to the divine world—into this trinity we as men are wrought. Our earthly existence is so shaped that there is nothing which we would not have to lay hold of with these three basic, human and divine faculties of ours. In the Ascension they are all summed up.

And thus, at the same time, this path is the fulfilling of the second request in the Lord's Prayer, "Thy kingdom come to us!" Usually in this request one thinks only of the kingdom that shall some day come from above. From this inadequate conception we are fully freed by our inward progress. We go the way of the Gospels themselves toward the divine kingdom : through death to resurrection. That is the way by which Christ Himself passed before us "into the kingdom." Through no outward door can one enter this kingdom, not through outward death alone. It is not a geographical kingdom, but a divine kingdom of the spirit. Strict conditions govern it : "Whither I go ye know, and the way ye know" (John xiv, 4.)

When Christ appeared to His disciples for the last time before His Ascension, He three times put to Peter the question : "Lovest thou Me?" One can feel, as one meditates upon this story, how this question each time penetrates more deeply into the soul, how, when it is received as a vital question, it melts the whole soul in a sacred fire. It is a unique means of self-transubstantiation, which Christ there gave to Peter, the earthly-minded. We may conclude our meditation upon the Ascension, and our whole series of meditations directed to the feelings, by experiencing as strongly as possible Christ standing there before us, asking this question. All that we experienced in the meditation upon the Resurrection is now in this Christ. And all that we gained in the meditation upon the Ascension and the Baptism is now in us. It is no presumption, but it is a fully-human appropriation of the Gospel story, if we, within this Christ, Who, radiant, encloses us like a figure which towers above us and enwraps us, receive into ourselves the question : "Lovest thou Me?" That is the question which always and everywhere sounds forth from His being, when we listen to Him. In the fire of this question, which has in it something heavenly which burns us, we are most fully re-created. With the highest heaven in our hearts, we then return to earth. "Father I will that the love wherewith thou hast loved me may be in them, and I in them." (John xvii, 26.)

154

IX

IN the three following studies we now turn to the training of the will. This has special importance for our time. In the will the ego works itself out. A strong will is a powerful protection against life which presses upon us from without, against weakness of the nerves within. The more life threatens us from without, so much the more powerfully must we learn to work from within. That is the help.

But now many things are in conspiracy to snatch away from man his will, which ought to be developing, especially in our time. On the one side, man's will is methodically mechanised in the great business enterprises. Apart from a few who stand at the head, men have but little room for the play of their own wills. On the other hand the will is systematically practised upon by suggestion through the great unions and parties. The individual gives up his own view and his own will because he cannot hope to attain anything without these great unions, and limits himself to the choice between the different parties and groups. In these two dangers we again see the Ahrimanic and the Luciferic principles working devastatingly upon humanity.

On the other hand a time in which the will is present in a human-superman way in huge agglomerations, is particularly suited to increase the will in the individual. He need only make the earnest resolve to undertake the struggle against the unspirituality of his time.

It is just in respect of the will that it is important to see exactly how far wills can be trained. In the Act of

Consecration of Man it says : " To Thee, Divine Ground of the world—I turn my willing ! May the power of this willing spring from feeling that unites itself with Christ, Who liveth in Thy life. . . ." It is in accordance with all the researches of modern psychology that only by way of the feeling can the will be called forth. One cannot simply pump will out of man. But one can, to continue the metaphor, let it rain until the kingdom of the earth overflows with springs. Thus have great agitators worked only upon feeling, and under certain circumstances have stopped and put on the brake when feeling is about to pass over into will—so that the will may break forth itself out of man so much the more elementally. An example is the famous speech of Anthony in Shakespeare's *Cæsar.*

It is to be expected that by our training of the feeling, the will of man will also be educated, and not only a purer will but a stronger will. But much remains to be said, especially in this connection. To anticipate, the will is trained by great aims, by great examples, by great hindrances.

Rudolf Steiner has often spoken of the Manichees. He described them as men who saw the real meaning of Christianity to be a sublime fight of light against darkness. They anticipated what only a later age would bring to completed development. Even as far as into the powers of a holy magic, they felt themselves to be the helpers of Christ against the might of the opponent of the Divine. They went straight against evil that they might wring from it the good, that they might transform evil itself into good. This divine alchemy was their Christianity. He who receives into himself these impulses sees upon the horizon of the future a Christianity arising, in comparison with which our present-day Christianity seems little and narrow. Not redemption from evil, but redemption of evil. Not changing men from evil to good, but changing evil itself into good.

A beginning of such a Christianity must be made in our time. This is revealed clearly to us, if we do not otherwise see it, by the secondary occult phenomena of our times. There are in America " metaphysical high schools," where Indian Yogis apply the old oriental wisdom about the schooling of the will to the preparation of men for activity in business. As the materialism of the West becomes dangerous when, as in Bolshevism, it is taken up by the forces of the East, which have quite different purposes, so the spiritualism of the East becomes thoroughly dangerous when it is taken up by the tendencies of western life, which are directed to the exploitation of the earth. We in middle Europe to-day stand confronted by this historical situation. In opposition to it we must develop towards the earth a new frame of mind which raises the West out of the dust. And we have to gain a new spiritual knowledge that surpasses that of the East. It cannot be doubted that a higher training of the will also belongs to our task.

All this is indeed the real sense of the Christianity which is now nearing us. This Christianity does not end with Heaven, but goes with Heaven back to earth. It works upon the earth, but with the forces of Heaven.

This is the great fundamental change which is being accomplished in Christianity to-day. Many movements, which are to-day vainly seeking after it, will on this path find their innermost religious basis and strength, socialism for example.

The great model for this Christianity is Christ Himself. And we acquire the training of the will which we need, when we look at the seven great acts by which the Gospel of John shows Christ's work among humanity being accomplished. We thus enter under the safest guidance into a holy magic to which belongs the future of Christianity.

In many ways such Christian magic is showing itself to-day, *e.g.* as prayer over the sick, as " spiritual healing," as thought-transference. We must come to an understanding of all these phenomena, most of which contain distortions of the truth, and must try to find courses of action which can rightly be put in their place.

At the end of the account of the marriage at Cana is found the saying : " This beginning of miracles did Jesus. . . . and manifested forth His glory, and His disciples believed on Him." To-day there is no meaning in merely " believing " on this " miracle," in the sense of an external belief in the Bible. How the event can have occurred, how it can be made comprehensible to the men of to-day in its historical reality—about this Rudolf Steiner has said the most important things in his lectures on the Gospel of John.

To us here this story is transparently revealing for the meaning of the whole of Christ's earthly work. Let no one think that in religious records such sayings as these are merely historical : " This *beginning* of miracles did Jesus. . . and manifested forth His glory." Certainly, one goes least astray if one takes such indications as hints, pointing to hidden depths of truth.

What was that meaning of Christ's earthly work ? He brought heaven to earth. One could also say : He made heaven earth. In past times men have been told about heaven. They have been promised heaven after death. And in Christianity this way of speaking rules nearly everywhere to-day. Political parties also promise men heaven, only it is a materialistic heaven upon earth. Christ went another way. He made heaven an earthly man, an earthly life, an earthly activity. In these three words we have also the three divisions of our studies in meditation : the "I ams," the stages of passion, the act of healing.

This cannot be said more briefly or more expressively than by saying, "He changed water into wine."

When the man of ancient times spoke of water, he did not think only of bathing or of sailing in a boat. He felt water to be religious. Water's power of purification was to him divine and worthy of veneration. In baptism still lives a remembrance of how man can dip into a purifying, revelation-bringing element. All laws and regulations about washing and purification are connected with this fundamental feeling. Man had above him a higher world which, through the water which it sent down from the heavens, received him again and again into its purifying forces. Instead of bathing, ancient man thought of religious purification, instead of sailing, he thought of crossing the stream after death or in initiation. The latter, the crossing of the stream, was the esoteric of ancient religions, the former, the purification, its exoteric. And so the old religious feeling lived with water. And when we notice what miserable remains— but still remains—of these feelings are alive in men to-day when they rejoice in water because of bathing and sailing, then we can perceive with our eyes what changes there have been.

Now let us look at the six stone water-pots, which "stood there after the manner of the purifying of the Jews." In this stands the whole of antiquity. In this stands the old religious existence of men.

But the man of past ages felt wine, too, religiously. Innumerable cults are to be understood only in this connection. The worshippers of Dionysius felt in the wine the god. It was a god that made man strong for earth, glad upon the earth, which separated him, indeed, from the delicate feelings for the spiritual world, which still lived in him from ancient times, but it made him glad in the experiencing of his own personality. Because man had to become a citizen of earth, he drank wine. In the juice of the grape the water of heaven is taken up into the earthly strength of the vine and becomes active as an earthly creature. Can one think of a more beautiful picture for that which Christ willed and was ? In Him the revelation from above is born as earthly being, earthly life, earthly activity. It is not without meaning that Christ appointed for the service of God upon earth, for the Lord's Supper, wine. He Himself was *the* wine. All earlier religion was water.

And so we may see humanity itself in the picture there described. They are gathered at a table. But they are in need. Christ came, and changed the water into wine.

How can this become for us a training of the will ?

The decisive union of the will with Christ is just this : that we decide to change heaven, so far as it is accessible to us, into earth, to live it out as an earthly human being in a life upon earth, in activity upon earth. Protestantism has thought less of " good works," and thinks that everything will come of itself, if it talks of faith. But this is faith in the full sense of the Bible : to unite oneself with Christ in a common will. " And his disciples believed in him." Not that we should obey individual commandments, but that we should become fundamentally one with him in will—that is what decides the issue. This fundamental will is revealed in the first great act of Christ.

" Repent (change your minds), the Kingdom of Heaven is at hand," runs the first announcement of Christ by John the Baptist. The fundamental changing of the mind consists in this, that one wills from heaven to earth and no longer away from the earth ; that one wills heaven but not for oneself, for one's own

160

blessedness, but for the sake of earth, that earth may be changed.

It is a basic mistake of even well-intentioned men, that they do not hold themselves bound to bring their " heaven " to all men. They keep it hid. Or they reveal it to chosen friends at rare times. Then they are not yet Christians in the sense that their wills are like Christ's will. Christ's will consists in giving to other men that which one has experienced in some higher world, or can bring down from it. One can feel oneself to be a thief if one keeps for oneself that which is given, " one thinks it robbery." (Phil. ii.) In this point the fundamental feeling of men requires a great transformation if it is to become Christ-like. And our meditation will help towards this.

Only there are two restrictions. It would be quite wrong to babble at once about what has been given us. We must first transform it within ourselves and let it work upon us so that afterwards we may be able to give it away. No self-satisfaction must mingle with the giving, only pure willingness to give. There is something horrible in discovering upon a divine gift to humanity the mark of the mediator's vanity. A white garment and on it stains from impure hands. We must be silent, as long as it is better for us to be so. Christ himself often said to those he healed, " Go hence and tell no man ! " This he did not simply to secure Himself against persecution. To others whom He healed He said, " Go and tell it to everyone ! " If one understands why Christ addressed the first saying to one and to another the second, one then understands an important secret of activity—to tell it to no one so long as oneself is immediately concerned in appropriating it, and to say it to every man when one has quite received it into oneself. That which is from heaven must come to men as if grown upon earth, like wine.

We can only point this out, and must leave it to our readers to think over life in its details, and shape it accordingly.

But, again, it is not meant that we should speak to everyone of our inner-most secrets. People would not be helped by that, and we ourselves would be injured. Much that is divine is not to be spoken of, but to be radiated forth. It wants to be received into our being so that it may stream out from it to men in power, in being, in silent speech. Also for man himself it is good that he may speak in this special way of divine things. He has the feeling that in such a way he speaks of the divine world more worthily, more truly, more fully humanly. He whose life has been touched by Christ will often have the feeling : I may speak of it only if I have first given to men *through my life* the feeling that they may hold what I say to be true. To speak of it may be only as the final word about a secret already revealed.

In all this lie possibilities and beauties for our life of which men know but little. If one sometimes lets the meditation pass in music into the thought—how would it be, how must it be, if that which I have now borne within me were to shine through my whole being; if men could read it straight out of my being ?—then would arise for us the world of which we are speaking here. It may come to pass, and it has often happened, that a man may see with elemental clarity into another's being, and feel that which lives in him and shines from him : That is Christ ! This will be the way in which Christ in the future will be revealed to many people. " *Thou* sayest that I am ! "—in the other man himself the voice first speaks.

All this means turning water into wine.

The divine revelation which we have received, first to transform it into earthly being, into earthly life, and let it thus transformed go forth from us once again.

The second restriction which exists is one which must be most carefully observed ; it is the duty of considering the needs and the powers of reception of the men to whom we speak. The higher a man reaches, the more strict is this law. One kills a part of one's own higher man if one does not act in accordance with it. For this higher man lives in secret union with other men. Never ought that which is divine to be spoken of so that we ourselves feel important in so speaking, or have any impure secondary aim. It may be spoken of only when, and in order that the other may receive a blessing from it. Speech first becomes something divinely beautiful and great if one has quite understood this command. No man can be used to announce the tidings, who has not the power to be silent until he may speak. Many would receive much more from the higher world if this were not a fact—that they cannot keep it for themselves. " Mine hour is not yet come," says Christ at the Marriage at Cana. This does not mean that one may not often say to a man something which he cannot understand at the time, something which he will at first resist. But such occasions do not do away with the fundamental rule, but only make its fulfilment harder.

Here we must point out something concerning such rules. Only in them is union with Christ's will completely possible. And the more we observe the true laws of life, the more we make meditation also active ; and we shall notice this in each successive meditation. We ourselves should become wine. We receive the divine blessing as the vine receives the rain. We let it ripen beneath the divine sun, till nothing remains but good fruits. But it is these fruits which we give as gifts to men ; not the rain which wets us ; not the sun which burns us and does its work upon us ; not the depths of the earth in which we are rooted ; not the fruits which

163

are still sour.   All these mistakes are made.   We bear in mind that Christ compared His disciples with vine branches, not with flowers, not with jewels, but with what is least noticeable, with vine branches.   He Himself is the vine, and we, only branches which have to lead the sap to the fruit.   Therefore it is not even the fruits which we ourselves bring that we should give, but the fruits which Christ in us brings.

To go still more thoroughly into the subject of our meditation :—

There are the men : humanity is assembled at the world's table.   They are in want.   Without Christ they must perish.   There are all kinds of ways of perishing. But Christ is there to give the true wine to men.   He brings heaven, and gives it to men as power on the earth and joy on the earth.   In earlier times men sought purification in the divine, now it becomes the giving of life through Christ.   Not only revelation, but food. This ought to be our will—with Christ to bring down what is possible out of the divine world into men's beings and men's lives.   We will work in the world like the vine which offers golden fruits to men.   We shall give ourselves to men as divine wine.   Quite a different feeling for life flows through a man if he can feel thus about the meaning of his own life.

In this meditation for the will, and in all those that follow, we leave it to the reader, still more than we did in the earlier meditations, to work out the details of the picture on which he meditates and to formulate for himself resolves of will.   The will is the most individual part of us and must be quite free.   We are giving, rather, brief glances at life and backgrounds for our mental outlook. But it is good to let the picture on which we meditate as exercise for the will act upon us in a threefold way : a great aim, a great example, a great resistance.

It is only another form of the same meditation which is part of the Act of Consecration of Man. At the words : " To Thee I turn my willing," the priest pours the wine into the cup. At the words : " May the power of this willing spring from feeling, that unites itself with Christ, Who liveth in Thy life," he pours the water into the wine. It is Christ, Who comes from the heights, as He unites Himself with the willing that has grown up on the earth.

Every right meditation is also a mingling of water and wine, or from another side, a changing of water and wine.

In the first miracle which Christ did, " and manifested forth His glory"—we have the first training of our will, drawing it upward from a small self-will to the great world-will. We stand again in the midst, between East and West. The *East* has indeed a divine will, but no will to change the world. The *West* has the will to change the world, but no divine will. Already over the first sign stands the prayer of all prayers : " Thy will be done *as* in the heavens, *so also* upon the earth ! " We pray this prayer no longer merely passively and no longer merely personally. We take into us the basic will of Christ. We begin *to become* " Heaven's " will.

The " other sign " that Jesus did was the healing of the nobleman's son (John iv, 46-54). And here now we see Christ engaged in a special activity, which had great significance in His life : in healing *sickness*.

If anything is to be done in this sphere, we must go especially cautiously to work, because in scarcely any other sphere is there such danger that egoism and materialism may thrust themselves in, as in the sphere of healing : materialism, to which the body is too important, and egoism, to whose heart its own comfort lies too near. This shows itself clearly in many phenomena of to-day, where there is the will to heal, but in no praiseworthy way. Against these two dangers the meditation based on Christ's second sign helps us. We begin in it to find once more that the story becomes transparent, so that we recognise in it a cosmic occurrence. The nobleman was probably a so-called heathen or half a heathen. At least, he is serving as a soldier in the non-Jewish world. There at that time the need was greatest. Humanity really lay dying. This was even true externally. Rudolf Steiner has told of a scene in the early history of Christ's activity : the young Jesus in His wanderings as carpenter beyond the boundaries of Palestine came to the site of an ancient temple. The sacrifice had fallen into decay. Men were plagued by a dreadful sickness. They beg Jesus to help them because they have come to have great trust in His being. But when He would help, He sees in spirit that here there have once been great acts of revelation, but now all is ruled by demons. The impression is so terrible that Jesus falls fainting. Such experiences, Rudolf Steiner tells us, prepared for the revelation in Christ, also for His activity as healer.

In the nobleman and his son, one sees in two generations the evolution of humanity itself. The father serves a king. Thus did men pay homage to an old wisdom which was given from above, and which was exercised by priest-kings. The son is sick unto death. In the father, the old heathendom comes in a picture to Christ and begs him for help. Christ at first refuses the help, or rather, waits until He sees real faith. The necessity for the new help must come from within. Then He speaks the word : " Thy son liveth." It is one hour past mid-day. The hour of humanity's meridian has just been passed.

It would be an entire misunderstanding of such thoughts to see in them cleverly thought out, or trifling, improving allegories. Everything in the life of Christ is heavy with meaning for the world's history. Out of everything, human fate is looking at us. And were we ourselves

166

filled with the divine in the events of our lives, the backgrounds of the world's being would everywhere come into view, our life and deeds would everywhere become symbolic happenings. All that passes away would, in a higher sense than Goethe meant, become a parable.

It is the wrong way round if we, because healing was a part of Christ's activity, rush straight at some sickness and want to heal it in the name of Christ. It is important that first we should see with clear eyes the world of sickness, the whole fullness of sickness, and the whole fearfulness of sickness. One must " lift up one's eyes " and receive into one's consciousness the terrible burden of sickness which lies torturingly upon humanity. Most men take serious notice of sickness only when they themselves are suffering under it, or when someone closely related to them has been struck down by it. That is far from being the true cosmic will. When Christ came upon earth, He found men distracted by thousand-fold suffering and in many acts He set His will with all its force against it.

The first thing that ought to rise up in us against the misery of sickness is the will. *All this ought not to exist in humanity !* All this belongs not to mankind but to the enemy of mankind. All this has nothing to do with Christ, but is to be overcome by Christ ! In Christ is the power which will, and can, make whole everything that " proves ill in earthly being ! " And first the only thing to be done is to see this fate of humanity clearly, not to pay attention merely to what is individual or our own, but to look at the whole, and to unite our will with the will which is in Christ, against the whole world of sickness, *so that the true Christ-Will against sickness may awake in us.* We take the side of Christ against the world. We feel Christ's healing power, out of which can come healing for all the sick in the world. We see in the son who lies there sick and in danger of dying, the picture of *the* human being ; we see in the father, who comes to Christ, the picture of *the* longing, and see in Christ, Who speaks the helping word, the picture of *the* healing. Simpler or more mighty the picture could not be. The more strongly the Christ-Will against sickness is present, so much the better is it for humanity, even if we cannot yet heal the smallest sickness.

At the end of the Act of Consecration of Man we hear three times the word " medicine." Again and again are the words " sick " and " whole " said in the prayers of this fourth part of the Act of Consecration of Man, in the Communion. That signifies that the nearer Christ comes to our body, the more He is felt simply to be health, to be mighty, healing health.

One can actually allow the will of Christ in meditation also to flow into one as health : and out of it feel with Christ how he became sorry for the people, how His eyes overflowed, how the power to help was opened in Him. With Christ against the world, ultimately, and in everything ; that is what we must be if we wish to achieve consecration of the will.

To be a healer, directly, through the real powers of Christ, is only possible to-day in exceptional cases. For it is required, not only special gifts and an especial guidance of destiny, but also, an especial call. And the possibilities of deceiving oneself and failing in the necessary conscientiousness and modesty are very great. An especial call must be there for every single occasion. Professionalism is just as great a danger as too great familiarity among men. And the truly Christian insight into the divine will for man and humanity, must ever illuminate such healing activity, and must become continually clearer. Otherwise serious harm would arise.

Every sickness has its especial duty in the life of the one who is attacked by it. Those who have the ultimate feeling of responsibility may heal only if they are in a position to procure in some other way for the person concerned, that which he ought to gain through his illness. If, for example, one wished to take away from a man who is given to debauchery his nervous sensitiveness, one would, in some circumstances, rob him of just that through which the fault in his character can be healed. This is often the case. Naturally the practical doctor of to-day cannot survey the whole net of a man's fate and the whole construction of his character. And even for the spiritual healers of the future, a complete survey will not always be the single requirement under which they may let their healing powers work. But the conscientiousness which must rule in this sphere must be stricter than anything which is to-day called conscience. No personal wish whatsoever must come into play, nor any personal apprehension, only pure obedience to the divine will and the strict resolve to act only according to a divine call which has been distinctly felt. If we have not *more* healers, that must be because humanity is not yet sufficiently trained for it. The pure streaming across of Christ's powers to heal is limitless. And we must dare to think such thoughts as these, if we take the commands of Christ Himself seriously, and desire to oppose the perverted phenomena of the times. It is exactly as a result of materialism and its development, that new illnesses will arise, against which the stronger powers of healing from within will be required. But only when the inward dispositions, of which we must speak more explicitly in regard to this sphere, are right, will blessing come.

Before a man himself wishes to heal, he must first allow himself to be very thoroughly healed. We have already had many cases in which real powers of healing have been received through the Act of Consecration of Man. This will increase appreciably in the future, the more strongly the priests fulfil the Act of Consecration of Man and the more strongly the congregation can receive it. But also in the most solitary meditation Christ can be active in His unrealised power to heal. At first perhaps one experiences it through feeling the places in one's own body where one is not completely healthy; then further in noticing that healing power is there, but cannot yet get in touch with the powers of sickness: then, perhaps, in remarking how the area of health in one's own being is growing greater, is purifying itself and strengthening itself, and, lastly, because at least certain symptoms of sickness fall away.

But even this, that one wishes to heal oneself of certain manifestations of sickness, and allows oneself to be healed of them, we would not advise at first, but rather that one should let Christ be present as health in mind and body, not in the body alone, and again, not in body and mind, but in mind and body; so that one feels: " Sick is the dwelling into which Thou enterest, but through Thy word my soul becomes whole."

Even in ordinary medicine, and in the cure of souls, one often advises men to live from that sphere of life which is whole in them, and that they should let this sphere of health grow greater and greater in them. We can think of such experiences when we feel health to be like a kingdom of soundness in us, which is always trying to extend itself, and in which we can live as in our central being. If one feels this so powerfully that one thinks that streams of living water go forth from us, that one has the feeling that one's very clothes must pour out healing, then one is on the way—in which one must now wait to see if one dare give bodily help to another.

In the early Christian church they healed by the laying-on of hands. And indeed one will notice how power to heal gathers itself in the hands, and will stream forth from them.

So-called Christian Science tries to overcome sickness simply by denying it, yes, simply by ignoring matter. That is a perversion of the truth, even if many healing results are attained by it. The right thing is always to approach sickness, even in one's ultimate feeling, as something which ought not to be ; as something which has only transitory value as a training ; as that to which Christ has opposed His being. If, in early Christian times, Christ, in His servants, still healed by the laying-on of hands, in later times at least the Host was still used as a medicine. And the decay of Christianity shows itself in this, that to-day, on the contrary, people fear to be infected in the Lord's Supper, and with individual cups and purifying cloths, try to avoid the germs of sickness. The very first thing we have to learn to-day is how to enter *every* sickroom in the right frame of mind, in no wise to fear the sickness, but also in no wise to consent to the sickness ; to bear about with us a surrounding sphere of healing, and out of this sphere unconsciously to spread around us strength and health, because we belong to the Saviour, the healer. In every single sickness we should see with eyes that penetrate and should fight against the whole world of sickness, against which the divine will itself is directed victoriously.

So again we stand between East and West ; between the *East*, which looks at sickness with fatalistic eyes and all too willingly leaves the field to it ; and the *West* which takes it too seriously, lives in fear of infection, fights externally and exclusively in a materialistic way against bacilli, and ends by falling sick through pure hygiene.

When one is near men who spread around them a Christ-filled atmosphere of health when they are in the room, one will usually feel for the first time what health is, in a stronger and more spiritual sense than men usually know health to-day. We shall not come again to a victorious Christianity if this activity is not there. As sunlight heals, so some day will the light of Christ heal.

We have thus before us in our meditation the picture of healing through Christ as an event which embraces the world, the father representing ancient humanity, the son, modern humanity, sickness as a fact of humanity, Christ as the great helper, and so, after we have brought all before us with intense vividness, we must pass over in our wills to Christ and experience with Him out of His soul, how the will breaks forth : *Thy Son lives !* So we become *one* will with Christ against the powers of destruction, and have not only life in Christ, but *create* with Christ's life.

In this it will be of the greatest importance if we always feel the *wonderful holiness of the will*. It is so characteristic of the men of our time that they dispute about the freedom of the will, quick-witted and penetrating, theorising and psychologising. But it is much more worth while to feel the *royal power of the will* in all its nobility. One cannot admire enough the Creator of the world, one might all too humanly say, because he had the courage to give to men a will that can will even against God Himself. This is the most divine gift which can come to men. By this above all He has made us kings and given us of His own divinity. Yet not too much strength of will ought to be given to man lest great evil should follow. But as it is, human will has the greatest future. And in union with Christ it may unfold itself, for certainly the Godhead has given its gifts, not for them to lie fallow, but to come to flower. Thankful joy over the sublime gift which is given to man, and over the trust which is shown in him, is the right mood in which to exercise the will. The will which is given to us is like *a call to a divine office in the universe*. " Holy is the will," let us ponder that within us, and become strong and glad because of it. "White will," one would like to say—as one, not without reason, speaks of "white magic." It is a gradual surging up of mighty divine power in men.

For all exercises of the will let still a double hint be added. The prayer for St. John the Baptist's Day in the Act of Consecration of Man speaks of "John who humbly bore the Father-spirit in the sphere of his body." Such words are, in their smallest details, not phrases, but the truest realities. Within the sphere of our bodies we find the cosmic will which bears us up. Out of this sphere we can draw it in, breathe it in meditatively. This is in accordance with the fact known to spiritual science, that the will is united to man more loosely and more freely than thinking, and even than feeling. As it were at the boundaries of our spiritual bodily existence the will enfolds us, which can be brought to our consciousness and enveloped into pure greatness. And as in the sphere surrounding the body, so it is also good to feel the will especially in our hands and feet. As something primally sound shall we experience this will, but also as something primally strong; in the feet more as the power to stand and walk, also in the spiritual sense; in the hands more as the power of creating and blessing, again taken in the spiritual sense. We shall feel the being of man's will to be richly articulated, and also find "right" and "left" to be different in hands and feet. With it all there opens up before us a premonition of the coming Christianity: to work with Christ as one Will against all the powers that destroy the world.

X

THE training of the will still languishes for the most part among humanity. The training of the mind is dilettante. The training of the feelings is chaotic. The training of the will is quite primitive. Every book in which one hopes to find something about this subject proves this.

And yet the increasing number of cases of sickness of the will—weakness of will, want of resolve, feeble vacillation—indicate that something must be done.

We must entirely reject all methods which approach this evil in too external a way. One can work upon the will by asceticism, by breathing exercises, and also by taking certain medicines. These can be a support to the organic foundations of the life of our will. But it is in accordance with the spirit of our time that the will should be built up out of the spiritual centre of the human being, out of the ego. Only so is it fully healthy and enduringly strong. It is certainly a help towards this if one freely gives up certain enjoyments. One will indeed notice how this concentrates and confirms one's will. But it must be a free renunciation, which has something of royalty in it, which *can* act at any moment, but *will* not, out of the nature of the spirit. Violence and rules from without easily bring about a damming-up of the will which is not quite healthy and which threatens a relapse. It was otherwise in earlier ages when the human ego was still only little developed. To-day the only safe renunciation is that which the ego renews at every moment out of its free insight. Such a renunciation is enormously refreshing for the life of the will.

We must also reject such training of the will as is offered us in the Jesuitical and similar exercises. It is not denied that they school and strengthen the will in a high degree. They break self-will. But they also break a man's own will. This is quite understandable because of the age in which they arose, and because of the object they were intended to serve. But they have no regard for the growing ego and its individual possibilities and tasks. They have no consideration for the ripening freedom in humanity. They do not see the royalty of a will which works out of an ego. So they develop, indeed the power of the will formally to a high degree, but at the price of having no free ego there to use this will. They put the man into a uniform. In this uniform he may feel his self to be strong, and believe himself to be something more than he really is. But nothing is more apt to lead humanity away from its goal than a spiritual uniform, at least in our age. In the exercises of the Jesuits, occult experiences of humanity are at work still with a thousand-year-old power, but they work upon an age that requires something different. They maintain the Middle Ages among us, even when through their pact with Modernism they fascinate many people. Besides much else which might be said about them—*e.g.*, that they proclaim Jesus the earthly king instead of Christ as Lord of the higher ego, that they overwhelm men with a whole system of dogma from the past, that they plant much egoism and materialism—this crippling of the free ego, out of which alone the will may break forth, is decisive for us. If to-day we bring to men new exercises for the will, much greater care must be taken for the individual value of each several ego. Otherwise there arises a powerful aggregate of will which can be guided by some power or other, but not the fullness of the Godhead which reveals itself in personalities whose egos are free. The dangers which are on this path must be overcome.

The third method, about which we shall not speak particularly here, is sport. One must indeed make much greater distinctions between sport and sport, than the layman thinks, who sees all kinds of sports represented in the Olympic Games of the present day. And nobody without bias can deny that there are exercises in sport which give beneficial training in self-restraint and self-esteem, which draw forth from the will power, swiftness, activity, endurance. That all this does not lead further than a certain restricted increase of bodily soundness, and of general self-control, can be clearly seen from the way in which those who are great in sport mostly disappear from notice in their daily occupations, without doing anything of importance in them. At the same time we are to-day inclined to under-estimate the less favourable aspects of the practice of sport, ambition, sensationalism, record-seeking, externality, unspirituality. The best that sport as it is practised to-day gives to the soul is the general training of humanity in good behaviour towards opponents, in self-restraint in the application of rules laid down, in respect for others in the battle of life. With regard to the practice of sport as it comes from the West, it would be necessary for the man of Middle Europe not simply to imitate it shamefacedly, but to think out the problem for himself and to place sport in its right place in human development. Then one would be able to discuss in another atmosphere how the attaining of a bodily goal gives firmness to the human will, because it sees with its own eyes what has been accomplished; how bodily tension and strengthening lay other foundations for the life of the will.

What we are here striving after is a training of the will from within. Rudolf Steiner recommended the following as a simple exercise : let one undertake to do something special to-morrow, something not so closely connected with the events of the day, but willed out of an entirely free will, e.g., to-morrow evening at seven o'clock I shall take a book from my book-strewn writing table, and put it in its place on the book-shelf. It may be also something apparently foolish, e.g., this evening at seven o'clock I shall stretch my arm out of the window. Such a meaningless action can be of this advantage that no force from without, not even through the reason, will be exercised upon the action, but the whole will proceed from entirely free will. One will notice how through such easy exercises, when one succeeds in letting them come forth out of the unconscious at the right hour, one comes to experience the royal strength of the will. And presages of the far future of humanity may play around such a small experience.

In another place Rudolf Steiner has shown that the bad habit of being unable to find things one has put away, cannot be combated by putting them regularly into the same place, but by exactly the reverse means, namely by putting them consciously always in different places, and trying to remember where it is that they are placed. There is no doubt that in a psychiatry of the future such simple methods will reveal a much more far-reaching action for good than one credits them with to-day.

Here we are striving for something else. And it is good if we first place before our souls the different kinds of will. There is a strong will that can press through with force against resistance, but is easily crippled, and there is a long will—the expression is Nietzsche's—which pursues its object over long spaces of time and grows stronger through contrary circumstances. There is a flexible will which adapts itself elastically to varied circumstances, and there is a rigid will which has no capability for changing its methods. There is a conscious will which lives in the clear light of knowledge, and there is an unconscious will of which we ourselves know nothing, although it governs our actions. There is the will of custom which works from taught or inherited complexes of the soul, and there is the will of opposition, which always wants something other than what is usual. There is the community will which is present in the individual with great force when it is shared with others, and there is the solitary will which loses pleasure in itself when another agrees with it. There is the direct will which strives towards its goal by the straightest path, and there is a crooked will which tries to reach its resolve by by-paths. There is the will of the outward world which never thinks that there is anything to be gained by inward conquest, and there is the will of the world within which prefers to leave all things outward as they were, so that it may strive towards its inward goal. Much could be said about all these. Our eyes must first be opened to all that exists in this sphere. Then we can better see into ourselves. The danger of the will is that it should become unspiritual, that it should continue to work in its own strength, even when the opinions from which it springs need to be changed. The will is also always unspiritual when it is not upborne by a deep insight. Especially unspiritual are the two errors in which we most often find the will; that it is materialistic or egotistic, or both. In the first case it lays too much emphasis upon what is earthly in the universe, in the second case it emphasises too much the individual ego. Here again are the Ahrimanic and the Luciferic errors which we have found everywhere. The ideal is a strong and long will which is every moment at the service of man, and which, while flexible to every condition, remains constantly set towards the highest aim.

We gain it when we consciously take into consideration the super-human powers of the adversary, when, over against them, we take Christ's goal into our wills, when we look upon the example of Christ. And so we greatly fulfil the universal law, that the will should grow by great aims, by great examples, by great opposition.

The strongest power of the adversary is called among men " evil." But one looks at " sin " in Christendom to-day almost exclusively from the point of view of forgiveness. However true that which is said about it may be, there is yet a conception of evil in which are revealed the ultimate heights and depths of Christianity. By it one recognises evil to be the power which exists so that good may come. Where there is no evil, there is in the strictest sense no good. Evil must grow to its entire greatness and terror, so that good may through them raise itself to complete power and greatness. If one can inwardly and deliberately oppose to evil the power of good, then it is possible to transform evil. And then the force of opposition is transformed into so much the greater force of divine goodness. He who has recognised evil in all its opposition to the divine has known God most deeply. He who has experienced evil in its furthest distance from God, best knows what love is. In him, who has borne within himself the full force of evil's rebellious opposition, undreamed-of powers of doing good can be released. Thus evil in the strictest sense acts in the development of man's mind, feelings and will.

The apostle Paul was often upon the track of such thoughts. He has dismissed questions which arise from them in the words, " Shall we then say (as we be slanderously reported, and as some affirm that we say), let us do

179

evil that good may come? whose damnation is just."
(Rom. iii, 8). His final decision is " Be not overcome of
evil, but overcome evil with good." (Rom. xii, 21.)
Paul could come to such thoughts only through that
which he saw in Christ : the Superiority of good to evil,
the ever mightier revelation of good by evil, the conquest
of evil by good, for example, in the soul of Judas, and in
the soul of Paul himself.

It was the Manichees, who, in connection with all that
was pictured in the Persian religion as the fight of the
light against the darkness, formed this sublime conception of evil, and so prepared for man a far future in
which such a Christianity would some day struggle into
being. According to Rudolf Steiner this will be based
upon the foundations which the being of the Russian
people offers to such a Christianity.

But already we have reached the time when there are
people who look at the world of evil in such a grandly
spiritual way, and who regard it not merely as that
which ought not to be, not merely as that which must be
forgiven, but as a world in which is buried an immeasurable fullness of deep knowledge of God, of transcendent
love of God and of heroic service for God. For this is
required a fearless glance which looks right into the eyes
of evil in its ultimate frightfulness ; a strong confidence,
firmly based upon the superiority of good over evil ; a
heroic resolve, which, in the face of the wickednesses of
the world, asks not only, like past ages, for a theodicy, a
vindication of God's justice, but itself takes in hand the
vindication of God, and accomplishes it through its own
acts, by bringing good out of evil. Such people, when
they are brought within the sphere of evil, find themselves exactly in the right place. They know that it is
just there that strong warriors for the good are needed.
They do not long for a world of outward peace and quiet

happiness so long as humanity is as it is. They shape their own actions, even when not much result can be observed, as a co-operation with the divine conquest of evil.

The basic perception of Rudolf Steiner, of which we have already often thought, is here illuminatingly helpful : that the might of the adversary of the world's evolving consists in two aberrations, on the one side the power which shuts men up in egoism, and, even in the form of a higher spirituality, makes him strive after his personal well-being, and on the other side, the power which draws man towards what is earthly, and holds him a prisoner in the earthly being with its heaviness and mental darkness.

These are the two powers which in the New Testament are clearly distinguished as being the tempter (diabolis) and the prince of this world (satanas). The more clearly a man sees these two basic powers, and knows them through and through, through their outward changes of dress and manifold disguises, the more clearly he feels himself to be in the world's service as a warrior for God. Such knowledge has nothing to do with ghostly super-stition about the devil ; it is an awakening to the world's background. One fights for man and for the earth " with principalities and powers," no longer " with flesh and blood." One knows that great wakefulness is required in the face of these powers. One feels that the victory over them is within us, that it is won decisively through Christ.

The fight of which we speak demands the highest heroism of which we as men are capable. If we seek for a picture for meditation by which we may bring it to life, we can, perhaps, at first, find nothing in the New Testa-ment which is quite suitable for us. We may think of the story of the Temptation. But because evil meets us in men first, and not in spirits, because it comes to us in men, as our inner sickness, and not, or not so much, as a conscious resistance, because men have rather fallen before evil than conspired with it, therefore our immediate task can be connected with the third " sign " of Christ in John's Gospel, with the healing of the impotent man. (John v, 1-16).

Paralysis has a close connection with humanity's sinful being which grows hardened in its earthly life. And Christ says expressly to the paralytic : " Sin no more, lest a worse thing come to thee." Here again one sees before one the nature of the old religions, as in a true picture, when one examines the description of the pool of Bethesda. The five porches were in ancient times connected with the five books of Moses, the Pentateuch. At all events, the men of the pre-Christian religions lived in fixed religious forms, as if in houses built for them. When they committed " sins "—in the house of their five senses, one might say—then there were washings and purifications, which freed them from their stains. Yet the strength of these healing powers diminished, just as there the power of the pool was now only small, and egoism entered into the nature of this religion just as there the sick selfishly strove against one another for the help afforded.

A new kind of help comes. " I say unto you ! " Christ often says this significantly in the Gospel. Out of the pure ego breaks forth the power which was formerly in the divinely troubled water. One must " believe in " this ego, that is to say : one must act according to the impression which one receives from it. Such faith in the " I am " is the power which fights victoriously with the earth-powers which draw us down, as well as with the powers of selfishness which entice us, with Satan as with the devil, with Ahriman, as well as with Lucifer.

One can find the two powers, and that which must be

182

brought against them, in the words which Christ speaks to the impotent man, " Rise,"—that is the power of raising upright which proceeds from the Ego of Christ, and attacks the downward-drawing powers of earth. " Take up thy bed and walk,"—that is the power of the new union with earth which opposes the enticing power of selfishness. What must proceed from us to oppose " sin " is just this twofold strength. We must look upon the " sinner " not as the bad man, but as the sick man. Therefore we must not strike him down, but raise him out of the dust of the earth. And therefore we must not merely free him from his infirmity, but help him to carry home his bed, to transform his fate into power. We must not reproach him, but must let the healing and helping powers act upon him. We must not merely proclaim forgiveness of sins, but we must let the powers of resurrection flow forth from us. Sin is *the* great paralysis of men. Whenever man allows to enter into himself the healing power which raises him up, it becomes the strength which helps him to carry the bed. We shall gradually come to recognise the entirely different relationship to " sin " which is expressed in these words.

And so we again stand between East and West. In the East all nature is felt to be sin, and they seek to release man entirely from his union with the earth. But in this they do not recognise the full seriousness of evil, which has ruined man's true nature and delivered him over to the deadly power of sickness. In the West they do not say that nature is sin, but rather they are inclined to conceive of all sin as natural and to excuse it, and so they deprive man of the seriousness of his position in the world. When from our own being there goes out the summons : " Rise, and walk in the power which thy past gives thee," when this echoes in our words and acts, then there lives in us a victorious relationship to evil. To him who lives in sexual error, as to the liar and the egoist and materialist this summons : " Rise and walk," is *the* message of Christ.

Thus we see humanity in the spirit before us, as it is described to us there (John v), as a multitude of blind, lame, deaf, withered, burdened with all kinds of diseases. We do not yet see them as a force consciously acting against God. For in most cases to-day men are not that, but a host of sick folk who cannot help themselves. They still live in old houses, which preceding ages have built for them. But the essential being of the ancient religion, represented to the senses in the pool Bethesda, " house of mercy," helps them little now. Instead of the water comes " the word." But the word must sound forth from the ego, and this ego must live from Christ. To know that the true warrior for the world is not here to beat down evil, but to raise things up out of evil, that is the first secret of Christ in the fight against the power of darkness. The second is this, not only to release the evil man from that under which he suffers, but to strengthen him by means of it, and so to redeem evil itself. Sins become destinies that teach : burdens become living power. " Rise ! take up thy bed and walk." Not much is said about sin, yet divine power so lives in us, and brings to pass once more that which happens in the child, but now in a spiritual and moral sense—rising and learning to walk. That is the right struggle against sin.

When we look upon this power which wills to work through us, we become free from Pharisaism, from boasting and from reproaching others. The more strongly evil comes against us, the greater is the demand made upon the power of the resurrection in us. That is a fundamentally different way of working upon evil from that of the law and the judge. Moses is no longer there, but Christ alone. In far distant centuries will come the whole great struggle against evil, when upon the side of evil, black magic will be more called into action. In that which is said here lies the germ of self-training in white magic.

Christianity will take quite a different place in the world when this frame of mind enters into men. And he who allows the words which Christ spoke in connection with these healing words (John v) to act upon himself, will form such a frame of mind more and more within himself.

It was in this way Christ Himself entered the worlds of evil. One need only look at such a story as that of Zacchæus (Luke xix) to recognise the characteristic features of Christ's fight. In it no word at all is said about Zacchæus's past. Everything takes place by revelation. But this revelation of His being cannot be resisted. Zacchæus raises himself out of his past by an act in which he transforms the past into a means of doing good. The same kind of thing is shown by Christ in the story of the woman taken in adultery, of the woman who was a sinner, of the prodigal son, and in many other stories. It may be a sublime setting free, to experience in a living way this method of Christ towards evil. Talk about sin is of secondary importance and often not necessary.

Where we see evil in the world, we may see always behind individual evils the huge world of evil, which must be fought, and may become conscious of our responsibility to share in this fight. Then we may, as we look to Christ, call to our remembrance the great watchword : the evil must be opposed through the two-fold power which from within raises men up and changes evil into life-force. And thus we stand rightly within the world-fight. In undreamed-of greatness, we can win this character of will through meditation.

If we would bring heaven to earth (first " sign "), let us oppose ourselves to the world of sickness and change it into health (second " sign "), let us oppose ourselves to the world of sin and change it into the power of resurrection (third " sign "). Now we meet a new world : the world of need. (John vi, 1-16.)

It is good for our time that we have also this story of the feeding of the five thousand by Christ. For our brothers of the proletariat ask above all : " What word have you for our need ? " They suffer from lack of the necessities of life, and look almost exclusively for some palliative for this need. That with which they reproach " Christians " is that they do not see this need, that when they do see it they do not take it seriously enough, that when they do take it seriously, the means by which they fight it are all too small. In respect of this, it is important to study such a story as that of the feeding of the five thousand. Christ sees the need. " Whence shall we buy bread that these may eat ? " He does not talk on the subject of how unimportant earthly goods are in comparison with heavenly goods. He does not blame the carelessness of the multitude which had not considered it necessary to provide themselves with food. He does not make His help subject to any condition. He *helps*. He sees men starving and gives them what they need, not merely what he thinks most necessary.

If men would look with the eyes of Christ upon the starving of men, the best thing would have been done for a solution of the social question. Or rather, the social question as it exists to-day would never have arisen. It is a reproach to Christianity that it has been so blind and weak amongst men. Is Christ's view really what is essential for social need ? We need only think of one fact, how rich and poor in the big cities have divided themselves into different districts. The rich could not live as they do if they had daily around them the need of the poor. They are obliged to create a protection for themselves so that they may not see what is there. Man can only be an egoist when he is voluntarily blind. In this lack of sincerity lies a deep consciousness of the solidarity of humanity. Every man, in some depths of his life, is so united to the others, that he can only be " happy " when he consciously or unconsciously uses a violent means of blinding himself.

Therefore this is a truly Christlike resolve : I will see the need where it is. This resolve is the confession of a frame of mind which will not be happy when it sees others unhappy. It raises itself above its own need, and lives with the common need. It finally abjures egoism and takes leave of every form of Christianity which separates the individual out of humanity for the sake of his own private blessedness. It feels instinctively—and this often makes a man shrink back—that one cannot rise to the full greatness of humanity's need, if one sees it really ; it feels that one must therefore be thankful if one does not see it all. For only thus one can live so as to help it. As much as we have within us the world of Christ, " heaven," so much of the world's need will we be able to take upon ourselves. This is not, then, " felicity " as men think of it in a sentimental and bourgeois way, but a higher world, which can live of itself, which can give and distribute itself. We shall not feel the urgent necessity of meditation until we feel daily that we must strengthen the heaven within us, so that we may not succumb to earth and its need. Then we can attack need ever more strongly, and cope with it more thoroughly.

Now, what has Christ really offered to men as a help against this need ? In this question we come to the actual difficulties of our story. All kinds of trivialities have been suggested as an explanation. For example, it has been said that the courageous faith in providence which Christ showed in making the people sit down, awaked in all who were present a feeling of brotherliness and a willingness to share, freed of all anxiety—and behold, there was enough. However little such an explanation may touch the kernel of the story, yet it may touch one side of the matter; and in any case in the social life of men one with another, there would usually be no need, if egoism and narrowness of heart, blind care and anxiety did not keep those hands closed which could give. In the Christian Community we have often found that in the cases of need, that which was required was already at hand, if one had only the courage to let "the morrow take thought for the thing of itself."

If we ask Rudolf Steiner (who alone, for our present time, knew how to speak suitably about these Bible stories) what really happened then, wherein consisted the unusual thing which must have happened, since they afterwards wished to make Christ a king, we learn that we have not to think of a miraculous increase of bread, but of a life-force proceeding from Christ, through which men are fed. Repeatedly already we have come near to this secret, that man can not only get the life-force which he requires out of his food, but also immediately out of the cosmos. If this is possible to-day to only a limited extent, yet phenomena such as Theresa of Konnersreuth* always point us to such facts.

It seems to us also that such a confession as the following must be taken quite seriously: " My meat is to do the will of Him that sent me." (John iv, 34). That Christ was not only fed Himself, but could feed others, even if

* She received the stigmata in 1927 and lived for months without having any food except Holy Communion.

only in an exceptional case, ought not for this reason to seem strange to us.

But through this we should come to a means of help which would be indignantly refused by the proletariat today. They would say : you point out to us, then, that there are spiritual things which ought to stay our hunger ! And thus you simply conceal the fact that you want to keep your material goods for yourself. It is certainly true that earthly goods become less important and less essential, when man can feed himself out of the spirit, but we must not stop short at this point, even for ourselves alone, if we want to live with our time and bring help. We must press deeper into the story.

Christ saw the need. And because He saw it and felt it acutely, He awakened in Himself the powers through which it could be overcome. Let us first stop at this quite general fact. Man has in himself an immeasurable fullness of possibilities. He has in himself every means by which all the need of humanity can be overcome. He must only will it. He has the means in his thinking spirit. And he has them in his helpful being. The Universe is a great kingdom of healing medicine, in which all the means of healing are present. Man must find them. This trust, that Christ in us brings forth from Himself the means of healing every need, if we really take this need into ourselves—as certainly as the human body, when it is strong enough, brings forth out of itself the means of curing every sickness—this trust we must awaken in ourselves. That gives no panacea against bad housing, against the difficulties of work and of marriage. We cannot expect to find that immediately in meditation, but we have the source of inspiration, from which comes all that we require, and with it we have much more than we can yet see.

189

And so we may arouse and strengthen ourselves for our social duties in the world by saying to ourselves in meditation : represent to yourself humanity as it lies there upon the mountain. Imagine the thousand entreating eyes and starving souls. Resolve, at sight of this picture, that you will never turn away your eyes from any need of humanity ; that you will look honestly at that which takes place within humanity, even if it should be a grief to you. Resolve that you will receive this need into a soul which is ready to meet human need, which thinks of it, which fights against it. Strengthen yourself in the confidence that Christ in you finds in His own being the means of healing need. Bring it to your consciousness, that in this spirit you have the centre of inspiration, out of which alone true help can come. Transform need into love ; not into blind momentary love, not into vain love of almsgiving, but into the healing spirit, which grows greater and stronger the more need surges round it—so, in your way, you will accomplish Christ's helping act upon the mountain, and find the highest which you can give to the need of mankind.

We can be certain that, even if no particular advice is given for such a meditation, we are doing the very best thing towards a solution of the social question. Round such a meditation a nucleus of " Christian Socialists " may be formed. An undreamed-of power may enter from it into our attitude to social questions : alertness, enthusiasm, endurance. A fullness of living inspiration can be born from it. A change may even begin in Christianity itself, so that men are more seized by the spirit of Christ, and the fight against social evils is not left to individuals and their slender means, nor to interested groups and their outward remedies, but undertaken in the sense of Christ's fight for the world. Not that Christianity loses itself in any particular politico-economic form of present-day Socialism, and thus stunts itself, but that it becomes a living power of will in all that happens in the fight against the great need of humanity.

We need a greater Christianity. We need a social Christianity. We need an active Christianity which enters into outward things. Here it is. Christ Himself is in it ; He will behold the need of humanity through our eyes, will move in our souls as the helper who overcomes need.

XI

Receive the Godhead right into your willing
And it comes down from off its cosmic throne.

THIS saying of Schiller, that most haughty-minded
poet, may stand as the motto above these last meditations on the training of the will. The Godhead rules
over us, just as long as it does not rule *in* us. But then
we rule with it. Out of this arises the royal attitude to
life which we receive from these meditations. Master
Eckehart once said that he would fain " in eternity work
God's works with Him." The proud feeling out of
which such words are spoken can be experienced in every
meditation which we here suggest for the will. Yes,
into this end and into this resolve every meditation may
die away. We can feel ourselves to be fellow-workers,
and friends of the gods. But it is just this feeling which
when we know our feeble strength, gives us due modesty.

Thus we give our answer to a question which is often
put : " Is it mysticism, then, which you recommend ? "
To-day people think that almost any sort of vague feeling
is " mysticism." But once mysticism was a serious way
to find the Divine Ground of the World, by absorption
within the soul, and to become one with Him. That is
possible, if man is able to shut out the impressions of the
senses. Then lofty feelings of happiness flood through
his inward soul. The mystics of all times tell of this.
But the divinity which man thus finds remains general.
Unity, infinity, blessedness ; these are the joys with
which the songs of the mystics are filled among all peoples
and in all centuries.

We are seeking in men not the soul but the ego. We are not seeking for this ego in obscure feelings, but we are striving for its illumination through the ego of Christ. We are not seeking for unity with the Ground of the World in blessedness, but for the filling of this ego with the divine cosmic will which is in Christ.

Another question is: "Where, then, is meditation spoken of in the New Testament? Christ speaks unequivocally and certainly about prayer only, and requires of His disciples only prayer."

To this question, which proceeds from the kind of Christianity which has worked hitherto, we have three answers. Everyone knows the words that are spoken about Mary: "Mary kept all these words and pondered them in her heart." What meditation is, can scarcely be more exactly said. One keeps a saying in one's soul and moves it about and moves oneself with it. A picture of this is the jewel which is moved about in the light of the sun, so that its peculiar qualities are revealed, and the sun becomes visible in it. If a man lets the saying of Christ: "I—am—the—light—of—the—world," move thus in his soul, and moves himself by it, if he lets it be present in his soul as the jewel is in the eye that gazes on it, then he meditates. This very saying concerning Mary can be a help to meditation.

We have a second answer. According to Luther's translation, Christ says in John's gospel: "If you will remain in my sayings, you are my true disciples." (A.V. "If ye continue in my word, then are ye my disciples indeed.") But the original text contains much more than this. Luther has praised the Gospel of John as being the "unique, gentle, chief of Gospels." But for the spiritual depths of this very John, a perception could not then be awakened. If we translate what stands there into our speech, we must say: "If you live in my word of life;

193

then are you in truth my disciples." More circumstantially still but also more penetratingly one might say : "If you have your abiding place in the divine, creative word, which is I, then are you in truth studious pupils of my ego."

The more deeply one concerns oneself with the Gospel of John, especially with Christ's words of farewell at the Last Supper, the more clearly it becomes apparent that Christ indicates as the way to heaven for His disciples His "Word," which is in accordance with the revelation of the "Word" at the beginning of the Gospel. But this is not only a word which will be proclaimed by preaching, but the word which echoes and creates in the soul, the word in which He Himself lives and works. It is a creative word, not only a word which announces. To meditate means nothing other than to let the "Word" be there, and to be there for the Word; to let the Word create, and to transform oneself in the Word. That is the fulfilment of the last commandment which Christ gave to His disciples, to go the way which He pointed out, to let the Christ live on in the soul.

But how are we to regard the Lord's Prayer, which Christ gave to His disciples as their new prayer ? Our third answer depends exactly on this point. The Lord's Prayer is decidedly a prayer for meditation. It is the ideal union of prayer and meditation. It is, in its whole nature, the direct training for that which stands before our souls as meditative prayer. Frieling, in his article on "The Construction of the Lord's Prayer," has spoken of this in relation to the first three petitions. It is really true that the earnest occupying of ourselves with the Lord's Prayer leads us directly into meditation. Then first of all we have the feeling that we would not wish always to pray the whole Lord's Prayer at once, let alone often and successively, but, quite on the contrary, to take rather one petition daily; yes, one of the three first petitions for a whole day, for a whole week long. Lastly we are completely penetrated by this frame of mind: Could I but once feel the first petition as it sounded in the soul of Christ! Then we labour to let the soul become such that it can really speak this petition, we let the petition itself work to this end. Then we are in the midst of meditation.

To Frieling's article I would add this: that it is fundamentally the same with the last petitions. Anyone who has read my sermons on the Lord's Prayer will see that, in occupying ourselves with the fourth petition: "Give us to-day our daily bread," we are led more and more to recognise that here we are praying, not so much for daily bread, as for the new man, who upon all sides stands rightly within practical life, who is armed with all the qualities necessary for everyday life. When I myself still knew little of what meditation is, this particular petition compelled me twenty-five years ago to bring it before the children in this way in religious instruction. But also with the petition, "Forgive us our trespasses as we forgive them that trespass against us": we shall soon notice in the second phrase of this petition, when we take it seriously, what sort of spiritual training this suggests. And that the first phrase: "Forgive us our trespasses" does not in the first instance call down divine forgiveness, but wishes to make it one's own, Luther pointed out. The request, "Lead us not into temptation," would likewise become more comprehensible to men, would give opportunity for fewer dogmatic questions and would come nearer to men, if it was taken in a more meditative way, if we saw in it less the expression of a wish than the contemplation of a divine spiritual truth: the realisation that we are led by God. Finally, the last petition: "Deliver us from evil." No one will believe that at his request it can be fulfilled between to-day and to-morrow.

195

A cosmic goal is set before us and a divine will experienced, to which one says "Yes" with one's whole being.

Yes, the Lord's Prayer is a prayer of meditation. By its whole nature it leads from simple asking to meditation—so to a higher form of prayer. Even if Christ did not use our word "meditate," His will is clear, His teaching is plain.

Men would be able to say less against meditation if they knew prayer better, *the* prayer above all, which is truly prayer, in which all prayer seeks to end—adoration. Of adoration as the end of cosmic history and as the life of heaven, the Apocalypse speaks sublimely.

If we would carry the training of the will further, an especially valuable and liberating exercise is connected with the next "sign" of Christ—the walking upon the sea. (John vi, 16-21.)

What happened to the disciples on that occasion? We must grasp this if our development of the will is to be effective. The people wished to make Christ a king. The disciples did not act with them. But neither could they be with Christ. When He withdrew from them upon the mountain, "Himself alone," that is a picture showing that He was lonely. Out of the folk-soul, out of the group-soul the disciples had freed themselves. They had not yet found the new connection. In such times, fear, and a feeling of loneliness, of deep inward unrest, falls upon the soul. Many a one may have experienced that, when he was obliged to break away from the views of his family and seek his way alone. He was like the disciples, who feel themselves tossed hither and thither in the stormy waves of life, and yet neither will nor can go back, but strive towards another shore which they do not yet see.

What appears in their souls may be summed up in one word, which includes again a great realm of need and of evil, the word weakness. Out of such weakness comes defective adherence to what one knows is true. Out of such weakness comes the feeling of loneliness. Out of such weakness comes that fear in many forms which rules among men, and torments souls more than is visible outwardly : fear of the future, fear of one's fellow men, especially of those who are stronger than we, fear of ourselves, and of that which lives deep in our souls, fear of sickness, or of events out of the usual, fear of death, and of one's fate after death, fear of all the unknown things that lie in wait around us. Maeterlink is a poet of this secret fear in men's soul. And only when one begins to be free from fear, does one see *how* the sickness of fear rages among men, and what disturbances, even of a bodily kind, it causes. Out of fear come the thousand shocks, small and great, conscious and unconscious, which make men ill and cripple their powers. Only if we know about this hidden need in men will we take the following exercise seriously enough.

But our question is first of all : How does one become free from fear ? Is there a complete freedom from fear ? We are not speaking of natural courage. In it is blindness, a feeling of madness, a feeling of bodily strength, a natural inclination, and so on. It is not secure against suddenly passing over into fear, when the eyes are opened to the real danger, or the natural powers on which it is based break down. I often think of the story of the two officers, one of whom said to the other in a time of danger: " But you are shaking, you are afraid ! " To which the other replied : " If you were half as afraid as I am, you would have run away long ago." Two fundamentally different kinds of bravery.

We can be free of fear under any circumstances only if we know we are quite safely protected, or if we have no concern for ourselves. Both are present if we have completely sacrificed our lower ego, and live for the higher ego. This ego and its existence is a concern of the divine world itself and not merely our personal concern. No one who has not experienced it can know the safety of this mood. " And were the world all devils o'er ! " People who feel that they are not miserably worthless, but rich in inward values, and yet in the greatest danger, live superior to every anxiety—these are the real fighters of this world. By such people the world can be lifted from its axis. All fear is melted away from them. They feel for the first time what freedom is. By this they learn the true nature of man, the nobility of the ego which does not pass away. How does one acquire such fearlessness ?

The story of the walking upon the sea is told us for that purpose. " It is I, be not afraid." It is known that the Greek text says simply : " I am, be not afraid." According to the English idiom it could not be translated differently, but the Greek text leads us deeper into reality. We lose every fear, when we look upon the " I am " of Christ, Who is willing to enter into the ship of our life. We can lay aside every fear of our life at the very moment when we stake our all upon this " I am." Men may shatter us and mangle us ; for the sake of this " I am " we live. Christ whose " I am " sounds within us, may maintain Himself in us, if He will. Life, the true battle of life, begins when this spirit lives in us.

But in the training of our will it is not the main thing that we ourselves should become fearless. That is only the primary condition that we must procure again and again. From every corner of our being we can seek out and drive away fear. But now it is necessary to come face to face with a humanity which is ravaged by secret fear, which cannot come to life because of a thousand weaknesses, which by inward unrest destroys its strength, and so cannot make its strength available for life.

And so we see before us in our meditation men as they are tossed hither and thither upon the stormy sea of life, like the disciples yonder in the boat; how in their anxiety and unrest they consume themselves, and weaken their lives, while trying to protect them. Such is the world. Such are men. And in the face of this we seek to live ourselves into the figure of Christ, Who walks upon the sea and Who says, " I am, fear not."

Let us here say plainly that we do not hold this to be an account of an outward event, but to be a vision of the disciples, seen with the spiritual senses which, after the distress of the night, unfold themselves towards morning in the disciples. The disciples saw a spiritual reality. They saw *the* spiritual reality. They saw the deep meaning of the appearance of Christ in the history of humanity. Thus they saw their own future task in the world. Outwardly there was nothing to be perceived here upon the sea. But the spiritual happening, not a mere picture of the fancy, was so much the more real. The billowing sea was not only around them, but in their own souls. But to these souls came the new ego, came Christ.

When a man who takes his share in this world's battles gives the impression that Christ is saying through him " I am! be not afraid," then men feel a benefit which makes their inmost part attentive. Nietzsche has spoken of a tree which refreshes a whole landscape. Here one must speak of a light which shines upon men, and all are aware through it of another world. The " I ams," if we continued to listen to them, would form this " I am " in us. We must really prove to men that we can walk upon the water. The unrest, the uncertainty, the stormy billows may be never so great; we are supported by a power from on high which bears us up. We have no firm ground under our feet, and yet we walk secure. For this cause there is the uncertainty of the morrow—

that we may have a chance of walking upon the sea. The resolve to let oneself be led by the ego of Christ, which comes from the world above, is the resolve to walk upon the sea—what Peter in the Gospels could not yet do. If we look again and again into this picture and see how Christ comes to the disciples over the sea, we see ever more clearly how men in their callings and in their families are travelling in a rocking boat. We see what it means to unite ourselves with Christ's appearing. The story is not a " comfort " which we personally receive, but a cosmic strength which we should receive. In individual cases we do not need to think of the picture at all. It works in us—unknown to ourselves, perhaps also unknown to others—if only we admit this Christ into our souls, let Him be there in our souls, " I am at peace with the world : this peace with the world can be with you also, because I give it to you ! "

Again we stand between East and West. The *East* will not put out upon the sea of life, because of its restlessness. The *West* will put out upon the sea, and knows no rest. We are upon the sea, but we have rest—not being far from the sea, but upon the sea—in Him who walks upon the sea.

From the practice of such exercises for the will as we here describe, a purification of the will will follow, which we could not expect beforehand, and have never known before. Then we look at the life of the will in men around us, and see how casual, how impure, how darkly unconscious, how eaten up by egoism it is. How petty as aims for the will are money, position, one's own house and garden, a peaceful evening of life ! And even these aims live only fluctuatingly in the thin wills of men of to-day. Now we begin to see how it is when a clearer, purer will lives in a man. By the great *aim*, which we take into our lives, our will itself acquires greatness, which works ever more strongly into our daily activities, into our momentary wishes. In the greatness of his aim, man himself acquires greatness. By the great *pattern* which we see before us, which is Christ, our will gains that fire which is not dangerous, to which we can dedicate ourselves entirely. We have only to guard this fire against the impure flame of fanaticism—which may be quite concealed. But through the great *opposition* upon which we look, our will gets the strength of steel. It grows into the super-human, because it unites itself with the super-human.

It is a world full of suffering, if we feel in the individual weakness of a man all the littleness, the lamentableness, the anxiety of soul, the lostness, the gnawing unrest, the dissatisfaction of humanity. Do not let yourselves be deceived : those who come forward with great pretensions of strength, and hurl around them arrogant words and actions are generally such men as are weak within. Often it surprises one to find suddenly—this man is afraid ! If one can get over one's annoyance, and does not linger over the resistance which is perhaps necessary, one is seized with pity for the weaknesses of these men, which they carefully conceal from themselves and others. Against this can be set up, without any arrogance or insincerity, the " I am " of Christ, as a power for victory which breaks in with radiance from another world. Just where men are really disturbed, as in a public meeting, one need only hold this " I am " strongly within one, and let it radiate out into the unrest. That is " pacifism " in the sense of Christ. For the saying, " Blessed are the peacemakers, for they shall be called the children of God," speaks in the original text of the *pacifici*, the *peacemakers*. They shall be called the " children of God," for such they *are*, because in unrest one sees that they are born from above.

If one can procure such revelations for men, they will see another Christ than the one preached to them. Our meditations will lead us to these heights. Tolstoi says somewhere: "I have only one wish: to fulfil the divine will; and only one fear: to neglect the divine will. When godly fear destroys all earthly fear, then man joins the army of the real warriors of the world."

That which we are here discussing is like passing the will through one consecration after another, to the real world battle. Thus we see yet another world appear, which is perhaps least of all seen in its need of redemption. This is the world of darkness.

Again it is necessary to lead our gaze to some of the facts around us before we can have the right impulse to meditation. Darkness, according to present-day views, is spread over the beginnings of humanity and of the earth; darkness over their goal, their meaning and their end; darkness over the destiny of the individual after death; darkness also over every individual appearance in its true being. In philosophy this has been expressed in the teaching that "the thing in itself" is always hidden from us. Never did humanity have so few and such uncertain thoughts about its origin and destiny as to-day. Do not more illnesses and suicides come from this than is admitted?

We must now turn to the training of our sight that it may see the darkness of the world. The men of the present day still live in a "dark age," darker in many respects than the "dark Middle Ages." And that they talk about enlightenment is a proof that they do not possess it. Even into theology, which ought to talk of the light, this world darkness spreads itself to-day. It ventures to speak only of the "unknown," "mysterious," "quite other" God. Thus it proclaims its need as if it were a virtue, and still asserts that religion has always consisted only in belief in this hidden power. He who closely examines what such a classical compendium as " Religion in History and at the Present Day " has to say about God and the higher world, will be astonished. That is hidden by many valuable individual items of historical knowledge. But in orthodox theology also, such as the theology of Barth, to which to-day many religious men turn, the world darkness continues to live, feebly illuminated by a few lamps taken from the Bible which are called " revelation." Men live to-day, without knowing it, as those live who dwell under the veil of smoke of a great city. They do not know that above it is a glorious world in which the light lives in a thousand beauties. They see clearly that which is beneath the curtain of cloud, but the worlds above do not exist for them.

In Plato's time men still felt the life of humanity in the way he described in his famous picture of the cave. Men live shut up in the dark, cast out from the real world. But upon the wall of their cave they see the shadows of those who pass by outside. To-day the cave is lit by electric light. They see clearly what is upon their walls. But the shadows of those who pass by outside they see no longer. That there could be another dwelling than this well-appointed cave, they do not know.

Certainly, there are riches in their cave : " Drink, O eyes, what your lashes will hold of the golden superfluity of the world ! " Gottfried Keller was the voice of men to-day, when he wrote these words, and Friedrich Nietzsche was the soul of men to-day, when he loved them.

But the increasing number of suicides reveals that men are not satisfied with this drink, good though it may taste. Goethe was a pioneer upon the way of humanity when he spoke these words through Faust : " Night seems more deeply deep to penetrate, but brightest light shines in the inward part." This same Faust, who was intoxicated with the glory of the world of the senses, seeks the inward light and values it, even when the outward eyes are surrounded with darkness. For he is not blind *now*, he was blind *before*. A wisdom which lights up the age is expressed in these words.

" And as Jesus passed by he saw a man which was blind from his birth " (John ix, 1). Everyone who comes into the world in these centuries is born blind. Christ was the light of the world. Christ wished his disciples to be the light of the world. His task, our task is to heal the blind. How does that come to pass ?

Many remarkable things can be found by close examination of the simple picture presented by this story. He who calls himself " the light of the world "—and that in connection with this action—yet does not immediately open the eye by saying, " Let there be light ! " but he goes the way the sun went, when it formed the human eye. The more closely we look at it, the more significant does this way appear. " He spat on the ground and made clay of the spittle and He anointed the eyes of the blind man with clay." Then he sent him to the pool of Siloam with the command, " Go, wash." With our present-day feelings of taste, we are shocked by such a story. With our concepts of natural science we are shocked by it. And we do not notice what sublime spiritual teaching speaks in this story for all those who feel the necessity of lightening the world's darkness.

Christ gives a piece of His life. The spirit lives more vividly and penetratingly in the watery element than in the material, as we saw in the story of the marriage at Cana. But Christ does not take water, as it comes from heaven, but water as it has passed through his earthly personality. Again, He does not use it as it is, but He unites it with the powers of the earth. But the healing does not follow immediately, an action is required from the blind man himself: that he should go to the pool of Siloam and wash himself there.

One can only say that this is an earthly picture of the working of deep wisdom. If we wish to heal a man of his earthly blindness, we have no other than heavenly wisdom. But this heavenly wisdom cannot be brought immediately to men. It only works in the right way when it has passed through our earthly personality. And this alone is not enough. The wisdom of the higher world must unite itself with the forces of the earth upon which we live, if it is really to help man. Only thus it becomes the true power of healing. Not as it may represent itself to the angels in heaven, but as it unites itself to earthly being, is it real help. And yet, we must not believe that the single act of another is sufficient, even if he were the greatest. Man must be brought to perform an action himself, and to go where complete healing is ready for him. The evangelist finds the name of the pool significant—*Sent*. That is the word which he himself always uses of Christ: "Him whom the Father hath sent." And so, in his significant speech, the evangelist tells us the ultimate truth: only if you purify yourself in Christ Himself shall you become able really to see.

Of course all such interpretations are absolutely painful to the man of to-day, with the intellect on which he prides himself. Yet it must be admitted that religious documents of past ages speak with double meaning in this way, apart from the hint which the evangelist himself gives. But now let us leave as an open question whether there was in the evangelist any knowledge or suspicion of these truths, and notice the mistakes made by men when they try to bring the light of truth into the darkness of the world. There are those who throw texts from the Bible at other people's heads, and think that that helps. There are others who throw scientific discoveries at the heads of ordinary people and call it "educating the people." Even Anthroposophical truths can be used in these attempts at healing. The results are notorious. A spiritual truth has power to heal, only when it has passed through a personality. It must have become a piece of a human life, if it is really to work. Abstract truths can be comprehended easily by thought, even when they come lifeless and stale to men. The truths of life do not reveal themselves unless they come out of a life. The more a lecture upon questions of life is penetrated in every sentence by the character of a fully human person, the more the life-sap of a man is perceptible in it, the more eagerly will it be taken in. This is true not only of lectures, it is true of every conversation. As a helper of men, one has often the primary impression—when one is giving advice—only when you let it appear that you have personal experience, do men take you in earnest. That is the first thing.

And this is not the whole. Men often go away uncomforted from a friend or pastor, and think : " What he has said may be all right and fit his own case, but it does not suit my circumstances, it cannot be fulfilled through what is possible to me." Only complete earthly activity gives complete earthly power. Personal wisdom must be added to life on earth. That which is to help must not only be truly and personally experienced but it must be brought to earth, it must be permeated by the earth on which we live. Very, very much remains theory and principle and never brings help and healing, in great or small things, because, although it is right and is perhaps worked out at great cost, it has failed to give earthly powers their due, and to allow them to work along with it. That is the second thing.

And the third thing must also be noticed. Enduring help and healing is only in Christ. To Him we must point, as well as we can, to Him we must lead, to the " Sent." He is the new world who heals the old. Otherwise there is only the single benefit, there is no lasting help. And he who is to be healed must himself perform this action, must purify himself in Christ.

We must know and ponder all this if we wish to be received into the ranks of the fighters for humanity in the sense of Christ. It helps us to meditate strongly. Christ's action as a parable, when we have once understood it, says everything, more shortly, more impressively, more instructively than many words. In the picture of the man born blind we see man before us, as he lives on the earth to-day. We see Christ before us as the light of the world. We see a truth which can prove itself in life in the help given by Christ, and in the way the help is given. Great worlds and truths and purposes will shine in through such a picture. When such pictures become transparent for us, the earth itself becomes transparent— and we ourselves are healed from the world-darkness. Christ lives in this story and out of it heals blindness to-day.

A time will come when men will not see before them stone and earth, hill and wood as to-day, but when all will be a transparent veil, soft and spiritual, and behind it they will see the working of the angels. To-day we are able to prepare only a little for this time. But still we can do a mighty thing. We can carry Christ in us like the sunlight of a new world. We can let him shine through our words, our bearing, our actions. So a higher world can flash forth before men, even if it happens only here and there. So the eyes gradually fit themselves to perceive another world. " The eye is formed by light for light," says Goethe, of the bodily eye. This process

is the type of that which must happen to-day. There is
"darkness upon the face of the deep," but "the spirit of
God moves upon the face of the waters."

In man himself this new "Let there be light!" must be
fulfilled. He himself must become translucent for it.
It is deeply moving to perceive this task : to become
translucent in one's earthly being and one's earthly life for
the light of Christ, so that the light of heaven shines into
the darkness of the world. Every revelation of man in
the world of the senses, even his movement, gains a new
meaning. Man can be the bearer of divine light, and thus
can shine through the world of sense everywhere from
within. Christus verus Luciferus—Christ the true light-
bearer—one must not only love this saying, one must
translate it into action.

It can only succeed if we concentrate wholly upon the
light in us, if we bring this light to all we are and do, so
that the light shines through it all ; if all that is earthly
exists for us only that it may be irradiated. That is the
fight of light against darkness, as it can be carried on
to-day.

Rembrandt represented in his whole artistic life the
battle of light with darkness. Goethe regarded with
reverence this battle of light with darkness as a worship-
ping of God. Our calling is to *be* this battle of light with
darkness, in all that we can bring into the dark world of
the senses by our life and actions.

Thus we place ourselves rightly between East and
West. The *East* has light, but not for the darkness. The
West has darkness, but not with the light. Christ is the
light in the darkness, and so are all in whom He really is.
"The light shines" again, "in the darkness."

We have spoken above of the glorious fact that we may
live out our ego before men, "I am, be not afraid!"
Now we recognise the glorious fact that a new world can

arise out of this ego, as out of a sun : " Let there be light ! "

Thus our meditation again trains us for the great world battle. The world of the senses becomes ever more wonderful when the light shines through it. Man is born blind " that the works of God should be made manifest in him " (John ix, 3).

XII

WE have now reached the crowning point of our
exercises for the will—Christ at the grave of
Lazarus. From death He wrests life. This is the summing up of all struggles. From sickness, health must be
won; from sin, resurrection; from need, love; from
weakness, faith; from darkness, light. From behind
all these worlds, death gazes at us, as the end of all. If
life is wrested from it, that is as if "heaven" were
brought to earth. With this, the new power of willing
began for us, therefore this seventh deed of Christ is really
the summing up and the climax of Christ's work.

Christ at the grave of Lazarus. To-day there are still
many people who do not know what to make of the
"miracle" of an awakening of the dead. Let them first
give heed to the little details of the story (John xi). How
Christ is deeply moved with sorrow for His friend, and
yet immediately attacks death; how the gravity of the
hour appals Him, and yet He does not for a moment
recoil; how He receives into His soul the mood of the
mourners, and at the same time speaks in words which
bear within them great cosmic decisions; how He feels
the individual event strongly, and yet with high resolve
looks into the eyes of the enemy of the human race; how
He carries His friend in His soul, and yet is full of light
from the "Father"; how He leads everything step by
step towards the final decision, how He, in the full power
of the conqueror, opposes Himself to death; all this is
already a picture which works on us so powerfully that it
awakens the last and best powers of our will—whatever

attitude one may take up to the story. One must not allow oneself to be weakened in the study of this picture by having in one's mind the anthroposophical conception: here an initiation is taking place which leads over from the old mysteries into the new time. For Lazarus was dead and would have remained dead, had Christ not come. It is a triumph of Christ's power of life which we are permitted to witness.

If we look at Christ as He stands before us in the story, it is as if a prisoner in our souls hears the voice of his liberator; as if the Gospel were continued in us; as if the call: "Lazarus, come forth!" sounded into the grave of our own being, and deep within it, something which we ourselves did not know was there, seeks to arise. An overwhelming love for Christ, for this Christ, can then stir in our souls. We feel that He is quite different from that which we had till now thought Him to be; more of a conqueror, more mighty in His strength, more majestic. This man or none—so our soul tells us—is the victor over death, the liberator of men who live "in darkness and in the shadow of death," the king of humanity. We feel in every limb to what battle between Christ and the powers of the enemy we are called by Him. We feel—this is *the* battle for man.

When we build up before us this picture for our meditation in its great principal features, we see in Lazarus man himself lying in the grave. It is indeed the end of the individual life, it is the end of humanity—if Christ is not there. The sickness under which humanity suffers, leads to death—and yet does not lead to death. The stone lies upon the grave. In this stone we see the picture of matter. Novalis uttered the remarkable saying: "The earth has hardened into stone out of fear for men." That the world seems to us so heavy, so dark, so impenetrably material, comes about because man has himself sunk down into matter. In Egypt once, as man sank more and more into this material earthly existence, they raised the stone upwards, as a prayer. Upon the same stone—Mount Sinai furnished from its spurs the stone with which the Egyptians raised their massive buildings— Moses wrote the divine commandment. But the Mosaic law itself lay like a stone upon mankind. "Who will take away the stone from the door of this grave?" That was humanity's question. All this, when we have brought it to life with feeling in our consciousness, lives in the picture we are studying. Round about this grave is mourning, the mourning of the world. We have already seen how doubt, Martha, and sorrow, Mary, are the two guardians of the world-grave.

Then Christ appears. We see Him as we have before described Him. From the heights of the worlds to the depths of the earth sounds the call: "Lazarus, come forth!" *He* says that who can say of Himself, "I am the resurrection and the life!" We ourselves arise out of the earthly grave. We unite ourselves to Him. We now stand with Him over against the grave—with Him we feel: Death ought not to be! Death in all its thousand forms must be vanquished! Into every corner of our being we fill ourselves with this divine willing! We shall be resurrection! We shall be awakeners!

At the end of our three series of studies we have again come to the resurrection. That is in accordance with the spirit of John's Gospel. That is in accordance with the will of Christ Himself. "There shall be no more death." "The last enemy that shall be destroyed is death."

It will certainly come once again that man will be able to awaken the dead. If already, the bringing of air, the outward stimulation of movement, the shaking of the body can call a man back to life, why should not the power of the spirit be able to do it—the power of the life which streams towards him ? Certainly it will be possible only in exceptional cases. But—can one not see the beginnings there already ? It can happen that joy may send to the dying a power which fills them with new life. It can happen that in crises which are already determined towards death the victory is won by the spiritual strength of a man. It can happen that a sick person, who according to all medical rules ought to be dead, can be kept alive, or can keep himself alive, by inward forces of health. That is not much. But were we so to enter the sick-room, the room of the dying, that we were filled to over-flowing with life, if Christ's power of resurrection itself were within us, then we should experience wonderful things. We should often have the impression that death was flying before his victor, whom he had recognised. But even if his prey could not be torn from him outwardly, he would withdraw as victor with worthless booty, and triumphal music would fill the room.

We may leave to the future that which man will yet experience in this way. But our meditation will strengthen in us the consciousness that man may not give up his arms in front of death, but must stand upright before death, must dare in the face of death, if he is to be man in the full sense of the word.

What we are first able to do, certainly able to do, is to beat down death within ourselves. Let us not believe that this has already happened when we have a general hope beyond the grave. It becomes possible, however, if we call death again and again to be our companion. That which many painters of earlier times, that which Boecklin represents in his portrait of himself, that we should have death beside us and make him our inspirer, that is the way to release ourselves from him—and him from us.

" Death is the means in nature's hands by which it may have the most possible of life." This saying of Goethe is beyond Buddha's power to say, because it is only possible upon Christian ground. It was spoken of the thousand-fold dying of nature. It must yet be recognised in its meaning for the inward life. When the last remnant of life has been wrung from death, then death can really enter into its rest. Death wishes to be the " friend " of man, not only when upon the death-bed he puts an end to the sorrows of life.

Mighty feelings of triumph are developed in man by death. He gives us concentrated power of life. The enemy, Death, becomes our friend in Life. To him who knows himself ready at any moment to pass over, quite freely, into the other world as soon as destiny calls, and who goes over the earth feeling : " During the next hour, the bullet of a murderer may hit me. Then, not because a human will, but because a divine will enters into my life, I would throw aside my body, and go freely into the other world : " to him death has become a " free death " in a higher sense than Nietzsche meant. For him victory resounds throughout his life. For him death and the transitoriness of this world are only the means of gaining true life. He returns unconquerable to the earth, with an exalted feeling of freedom.

All this slumbers in the depths of our meditation. We cannot gain these heights in life more certainly than when we unite ourselves with the victor's will that makes Lazarus a John. We see inwardly into Christ, Who afterwards Himself broke through death.

But still more rests in our meditation. When Christ says, " Let the dead bury the dead, but go thou and pro-claim the kingdom of God," one sees clearly that He felt the living around Him to be dead. The saying con-cerning the kingdom of God is a call to life which sounds into the kingdom of the dead. We do not exist simply to continue to exist personally after death, but chiefly to conquer death. Deceitful appearances of life conceal death everywhere. Painted in the colours of life the dead go about in the world. All this death, which we see in countless forms upon the earth, calls for life. When we fill ourselves to the brim with the streams of life, when we go into the world as life itself embodied, then we shall rightly see this death in its thousand changes of dress, and go to meet it as the call to life.

Again we may look at East and West in order to awake to the greatness of our calling. In the East they saw death with sublime clearness. In all the bloom of life lurks the germ of destruction. This view of the awakened East is deeper than the view of the West. But the will of the West is more in the right than the will of the East.

In the East they wish to escape from the earth whose ruler is death. In the West they wish not themselves, but death, to be taken from the earth. But death is attacked by completely inadequate means. They fight with rejuvenating methods and hygiene. They fight feebly with all kinds of attempts to turn death aside. They will not face death, or they push him away as long as they can. To see what the East sees, to will what the West wills, but to be able to do what East and West cannot do : that is our mission.

It is an awakening of the dead also when in life we summon ourselves again to see in every man his spiritual being, when we look through the form, the bearing, the words of a man to his real ego. Even for this is required more spiritual power and unwearied will to life than we can usually summon up in our lives. In our meditation we shall grow into this will and into this power. We shall then experience that men feel for the first time that they are being rightly treated by us.

We have reached a further height when we go with awakening power through nature. We see in it not death, but the spirit ; not the earthly kind, but the divine image ; not what passes away, but a message from higher kingdoms. Every plant can be so regarded. We shall not reach this by a single resolve. In one single walk we can guess at it. But we can strengthen ourselves for this and exercise ourselves in it, if at times we call plants also into our meditation, look at a rose, a lily spiritually, and listen for the revelation which comes to us in them. If we then go out into nature, it will often be as if a rejoicing over redemption passed through the world, as if the world around us would become such as lives in the spiritual world, as if we ourselves walked in Paradise. Christ is the awakener of the dead. We ought to have the courage to be this with Him as strongly as we can.

There is one sphere especially in which we must not let death have any influence : that of our departed. Now we stand before a question which is most often put : What can we do for our dead in meditation ?

One can give no better advice to those who wish for a thorough investigation of this question than that they should study the lecture cycles of Rudolf Steiner. Rudolf Steiner's assertions in this sphere also, are not intended to be taken as dogmatic, but to be thought over and tested by all the knowledge possible to us. The fullness of illumination on the subject of life after death which has broken in upon us through Rudolf Steiner, is a cause of ever-renewed astonishment to everyone who can make a survey of it, even to a small extent. Here some introductory remarks only will be made. One should always draw near to one's dead in a mood of solemn restfulness, not with restless wishes or in an egotistical mood, but in thankfulness that they have existed. This will best come about if one remembers the hours when one was with them in quiet human friendliness. The basic feeling ought to be : live peacefully there looking upwards ! I shall fight my way through upon earth. From me shall naught come to thee but love, which bears thee up from below when thou art living towards the light above ! Only as good shall this love be around thee ! I will tell thee not of my troubles, but of the joys which I have experienced, of the spiritual good that has come to me. Such love is like a bridge of light which we build to the dead, upon which we can come to them and they to us. First of all, a feeling of community with them will arise. We shall feel ourselves near to them in the night, when the noise of the day within us and around us is silent. We shall wake in the morning with the feeling as if we had been united with them and had walked with them in high places. Then we shall sometimes have the feeling of their nearness during the day. Perhaps when we turn our attention to this feeling, it will have already gone away. But the feeling that they help us is such a wonderful enrichment of our life that even a few presentiments of this kind change it wholly. We learn to know a depth, a nearness and beauty of fellowship of which we had previously been unconscious. An unheard-of future for humanity arises before our sight, in which life is passed in a working together of the living with the dead, and of the dead with the living.

The opposite of this occurs in spiritualistic seances, sultry, ghostly, and demonic. The mediums do not reach our dead, because they themselves pass into a lower condition of soul life, into a half-conscious or unconscious twilight condition, while our dead live in brighter fullness of life. Thus the mediums come only into the kingdom where are the sheaths which our dead have laid aside. Therefore they bring from thence only absurd phrases which tell us nothing, mixed perhaps with memories of the past life, and vague imaginings. If we really reached our dead through these mediums, these egotistical questions and wishes for the dead would be only a severe disturbance and injury to them in the tasks they now have. There is indeed a way of questioning the dead, but it is to send them our questions in perfect quietude, as we go to sleep in the evening and to seek to feel on awakening in the morning the answer that is in our souls. All this should be in that pure sphere we have described above : " I am the door."

If we should succeed in feeling that death is nothing in respect of our friends who have gone, and that we live on with them as with people who have not gone away, but have gone before us, so that we bear them in a pure world of life within our souls, then we shall have the impression that by this attitude we are helping them. Even when we can find no special relationship to them in details, yet if we let their form, their look, their voice, their best selves live and work in our remembrance, we shall have the experience of a higher form of fellowship. We make no distinction between living and dead. We know living who are dead, and dead who are alive. Since we often feel the existence of the dead more purely and strongly than the existence of the living, we give to them actually the possibility of sharing our life. We awake the dead. Our meditation helps us to this.

In the five kingdoms of need, we have before us all that must be overcome upon earth. Now in the last exercise nothing remains but life : heaven upon earth. That which the first exercise for the will awakened in us as a common aim for life has now been fully unfolded.

We practise all these exercises for the will in such a way that we first place the individual historical picture vividly before our souls. Through the need in the individual picture we see the world's need, the mighty kingdom of evil that must be overcome. We ask ourselves if we really will earnestly that this opposing world shall be overcome. We answer this question with our whole will. Thus our will acquires the greatness which acts more and more upon our everyday wishes. But now we call to life within us the example of Christ. In Him heaven fights for earth. We enlist on His side against the whole world. As if from the other world we work with Him. With our ego and with our best selves we are already beyond the grave. Our " citizenship " as the Bible says, is in a higher world. As we look at Christ our will gains the pure, fiery essence, the true, divine warmth. But the more we see in the details, see in the small things the greatest and last things, the decisive struggle for the world, so much the more does our will gain the strong power through meeting great obstacles. And thus again in each single exercise we go the way from the spirit, through feeling to willing : from the great aim, through the great example, to the great power.

This means to live in the spirit of Michael ! To work in the spirit of the Archangel who was always regarded as the great champion of Christ in the earthly world. We should ever renew our resolve to think and work in the world in the spirit of Michael. The spirit of the age demands this of us. It means also : to live apocalyptically.

At the end of such an exercise one may retain only the will, and feel it in all its greatness, warmth and power. The earthly kingliness of such a will streams through us. But we feel it, not only as coming upwards from beneath, but above all as coming down from above. It reveals itself as the noblest sap of the life of the divine which wills to work in us. Especially when we feel in this will the being of Christ shall we have such an experience. One can let this will stream out from the head, in which one gathers it together in the middle of the forehead, throughout our whole physical body, throughout our whole spiritual body. What a " spiritual will " is, as the wedding ritual of the Christian Community puts it, we shall then experience. And we can attempt this also : to let such a will flood through us out into the world. Thus Buddha in his meditation sent out sympathy in all four directions. Thus Christ said, " I am come to send fire on the earth ; and what will I, if it be already kindled ? " Even when with this will we can will and accomplish no particular thing, yet we can let this good will be in us and stream out from us. By this we can learn still better how to " pour," as the Act of Consecration of Man says, " good will into our words and acts." Through this we procure divine power to create new possibilities. Our will is a spiritual reality which is offered, is sacrificed to the higher powers, which will the Good. Only in a close communion of life with Christ can any step be taken which ought to be taken in the service of a renewal of the world. Even he who has not yet regarded Christ as a divine personality will, out of all this, be able to take for himself that which he can do in order to become strong in the service of what is good.

Since to-day all kinds of occultism are showing themselves among us, let us here point this way to a white magic. In all details the following guiding lines must be observed : strict fidelity to truth, respect for all men's freedom, and a striving for the perfecting of the world in the spiritual goodness which is in Christ. The safeguard against all misuse lies in the prayer : " Thy will be done on earth as it is in the heavens." In this prayer we have now conquered the passive tolerance, the egotistical narrowness, which is so often put into it by men. We have led it upwards to the heights upon which it was lived out in the Gospels. If we allow Christ Himself to pray it in us, we can bring to a close our exercises for the will, as we summed up our exercises for the spirit in the prayer: " Hallowed be Thy name," and our exercises for the feelings in the prayer: "Thy kingdom come."

When we now survey the whole, the question comes to us : who will really go the way which is here described ? Possibly few. But these letters may become a help to religious development, even when one only reads in them from time to time and allows oneself to be touched by the spirit of Transubstantiation out of which they were born.

But we will take courage to go to the end, to speak for the few who will wish to draw from this book something stronger to help their self-training. They will ask, " How shall we best take all this into our lives ? "

To this we should like again to repeat and lay down more definitely this piece of advice, that it is good three times a day to enter into the highest. For many it will be hardest to find rest and time at the midday hour. He who is able might dedicate to the training of his higher self a quarter of an hour in the morning and evening, and at least a few minutes if not a quarter of an hour at midday. Still better would be at morning and evening half-an-hour, and at midday at least a quarter of an hour.

These times of the day are completely different. We cannot describe the difference more clearly than in connection with the Christian conception of the Trinity. Let us begin the day with the evening. At evening time, when a man must give himself over in trust to the powers of the night, he is nearest to the divine power which holds and bears up all, which has given him the body, and has restored it; into which he sinks at death as well as in sleep. An abysmal trust, a perception of hidden glory, a feeling of union with the ultimate source of all being, will then spread itself over his soul. It is one of the most intimate experiences of meditation that we meditate best in the evening, as if from the cosmic sound of the Divine Father.

The morning is quite different. It is a solemn experience to feel the flashing up of the ego in the human body. One is again upon the earth. One returns to the earth. In this alone there is something Christ-like. In wonderful purity one can hear the voice of one's higher being.

In it is our higher ego, which is united with Christ. We are ourselves new-born every morning. We become a son. We become also a sun. The light dawns in us, as it has dawned around us. We can feel in the morning that during the night we have been in spiritual regions, but that Christ must be sought upon earth. Here He has His work. Thus the morning meditations are strongest and most successful when we meditate out of the cosmic sound of the Divine Son. That which we have just expressed need not always be thought out in detail. But it helps us to discover this sphere of life.

But at midday the sun shines hottest. Life is oppressive. We are in the midst of material existence. It is hardest for us to get out of it. We must call the Spirit to our aid, must awaken ourselves to the Spirit. One can have this feeling : just as outside everything is lying in brightest light, so must you let still clearer light shine into yourself, if you will be great enough for your day. Spirit, Holy Spirit against matter, against the illusion of the senses. Humanity has placed the festival of the Holy Spirit near St. John the Baptist's day, when the sun shines most brightly. In this is expressed the same need that we met just now in our meditation. When we are in a position deliberately to place over against the outward brightness the light that radiates forth the Spirit, when our looking upon the world is permeated by the light of the Spirit, then shall we first know what the Holy Spirit is. Therefore we ought not to omit at midda[...] meditation at least so far that we do n[...] sound in our life.

These things of which we speak he[...] shades in life than are common to th[...] this passing through the three spheres, this daily baptism in the three worlds of God, contains something which blesses marvellously. It raises life to a sublime height. It crowns man with divinity. And man will learn that in the night he is taken up into the unity of the Three, that he experiences like music the community and interpenetration of the three divine worlds. He then lives in the Divine Ground of the World. He is seen, he is blessed, he is meditated, as he himself has meditated. After he has by day, according to the law of the earth, passed successively through the three worlds, he feels himself in the night to be beheld by a primal divinity, whose life he shares. He may live in this unity, even if only vague perceptions of this occurrence of the night shine into his day-consciousness.

The year also, in the same way as the day, is in itself living. If we would carry through the meditations in connection with the course of the year, then from Advent through Christmas time to the beginning of Lent the " I ams " are nearest to the soul. The outward world sinks into darkness. So much the brighter shines the light within. On Christmas night and during the twelve holy nights, the " I am " shines in the darkness of the world with spiritual power. When the Passion weeks begin, and up to Ascension and Whitsuntide, is the time when the meditations from the Washing of the Feet up to the Resurrection and Ascension are naturally fitted into the course of the year. The outward sun is then sacrificing itself to the earth. And man answers it with an inward course of sacrifice. Passiontide and Spring, seeming contradictions, chime together when one looks at the spiritual. But for the meditations for the will, the best time is towards Autumn when the days grow shorter, when man must oppose greater inward force to the decreasing of the outward light, to the dying of the earth, when he feels that now Michael will become his spiritual protector in order that he may not sink down into the sadness of the world which is breaking upon him, that he may bring forth the inward Easter as answer to the outward Easter which was proclaimed to him half a year before.

All this need not be practised by rule. In a high degree man can make himself independent of the course of the year. It would be well, especially, if a man once went slowly through all the exercises, even if it took years. He may remain at each individual exercise until he grasps its meaning and has won its first blessing. He will then most quickly come to feel the benefit and scope of the whole.

But once again, in conclusion, be it said—Someone may remain at the two first exercises, " I am love " and " I am peace," all the days of his life, and let the others serve as the illumination and filling out of these two fundamental exercises. In any case it is good that one should *never* give up these two meditations but bear them always as basic elements in one's soul. It is actually true that these two meditations bring about a communion, a receiving of the body and blood of Christ, as we have explained. We have in them, in higher form, that which was in the old mysteries awakened in the soul as pity and fear. Aristotle says that about tragedy. Through them the Mysteries work openly. Out of fear comes reverent worship. Out of pity comes love that streams forth. That is the inward frame of mind in which the body and blood of Christ give themselves to us.

If anyone should feel the need of having in addition to the meditation " I am peace " in the evening, and " I am love " in the morning, a meditation of the same kind for midday, it would be : " I am the word," thought of as a creative spiritual act. This would unite us to the Holy Spirit in the same way as peace unites us to the Father and love to the Son.

When I wrote these letters, I had before me the picture of a far future. I thought how Rudolf Steiner spoke of the spiritual character of a Russian culture which is to come, which is to be expected only after many centuries. Then, indeed, one will be able to say much better things than in these letters. On the other hand, not even that which is here described is entirely possible in our time. Ought one therefore to leave it unspoken ? When I had already almost resolved to do this, I saw that it was not permitted. Then let it go forth and itself seek out the people to whom it means anything. For many, perhaps, it is already valuable to see that there can be a life quite different from that which they live to-day, and to recognise that this life need not be led in cloisters and hermitages, but that the strength of inwardness can be built up in active outward life.

Then let us say one last thing. We connect it with a great symbolic figure in world-history which has been handed down to us from ancient times, the Sphinx. Through Rudolf Steiner we have heard that in the figure of the Sphinx there stands before us the emerging of man from the animal world, more spiritually than it is present in the ideas of present-day science. That which in the animal world exists as the eagle's capacity to raise itself from the earth, as the power of flight to the sun, has been changed by man within himself to the power of the spirit, to the will to strive upwards, high above the earthly. That which in the animal world exists as the lion's courage, as instinctive leaping passion, that has man spiritualised to the capacity for noble feeling; that which in the animal world lives as the bull's strength, as physical energy and external impetuosity, that man could change into spiritual will. In ancient times, according to Rudolf Steiner, they tried in the Mysteries to see to which kingdom men's powers were most nearly related, and then trained the pupils of the Mysteries to be sages if they bore within themselves principally the eagle-powers of the spirit; or to be physicians if the capacity for feeling was the ruling force in them; or to be magicians, if one trusted their power of will. But those in whom these three gifts were balanced were men in an especial sense. In the symbols given to the four evangelists these perceptions drawn from the Mysteries still work.

One may regard this as only a historical picture. Even then it makes clear to us from a new side the training for humanity which we are here seeking with the help of John's Gospel. It is the highest wisdom which comes into being for us out of these " I ams." In our age, when harm is being done in the great cities by so-called Yoga teachers, when exercises are being spread broadcast whose motive power is the egotism of social ambition, of the acquisition of strength and of superiority, wisdom in its bright purity lives in these " I ams." He who builds this temple around him will have the feeling that he has a sheltering spiritual home. All occult practices whose meaning and aim one cannot completely perceive, ought to be strongly discouraged. If anyone seeks a reliable guidance into the occult realms, one can recommend only the books of Rudolf Steiner, *e.g.* " Knowledge of Higher Worlds and its Attainment " and " An Outline of Occult Science." Here rules the spirit which alone may lead us in this realm : selfless seeking for the spiritual basis of the world, the attainment of accord with the moral order of the world, the applying of the will, not to subjective efforts, but towards the divine goal of the world. Only in such a spirit can one enter the occult realm without danger. Our exercises do not combat this, they train for it. To have the spirit of the wisdom of the " I am " shining around one, is more important and gives more illumination to one's actual life than if one tried to compel by doubtful means the reception of impressions from hidden worlds. If here we are trying to educate the " wise man," there is also a training, suited to the time, for the " healer." It takes place here in connection with the revelation of Christ in Passion and Resurrection. It lies not in surging feeling, in which we feel ourselves happy, but in a mood, essential for life, which is born out of the sacrificial spirit of divine love. So comes into being true goodness which brings healing to the world.

But our exercises for the will, in connection with the working of Christ Himself, train us for playing our part with mighty powers of will in that battle for the world which is awaited by the divine powers, and raise us to be real fellow-workers with the Godhead. Out of Christ's earthly actions we draw powers to train us to a new " white magic." That these are the same powers which live in the seven sacraments of the Christian Community can only be indicated here. If one looks at these sacraments, or as we might also say, these supersensible acts of Christ, in the following order : Baptism, Confirmation, Confession, The Lord's Supper, Marriage, the Consecration of Priests, Extreme Unction, then there works on in them that which was once active in the seven great acts.

Perhaps some will need a longer time to become familiar with this world of the sacraments. Our aim might be to fill, through these exercises, the three first petitions of the Lord's Prayer with the rich content of the Gospels themselves. In unison with the Lord's Prayer, the spirit of Christ itself seals us with that which we are here trying to do :—

> Hallowed be Thy name
> Thy kingdom come,
> Thy will be done
> On earth as it is in Heaven.

The course of the Act of Consecration of Man corresponds in the same way to our exercises : from the Word to the Sacrifice, and through the Transubstantiation to the Communion, the ultimate re-union.

Thus we can feel ourselves enfolded in the radiant form of Christ, and in it live our lives.